THE
BREES
WAY

The best of my hundreds
of interviews with #9
complemented with
perspective from those
who know him best

MIKE NABORS

CRTTT Publishing
Tampa, FL

The Brees Way
By Mike Nabors

CRTTT
PUBLISHING

CRTTT Publishing
Tampa, FL

Cover Photography: Parker Waters
Editor: Roy Cummings
Book Cover Design and Interior Layout: Kendra Cagle

Library of Congress Control Number: 2021950780

ISBN: 978-0-578-31068-8 (paperback)
         978-0-578-31333-7 (ebook)

DEDICATION

This book is dedicated to my daughters Morgan and Ally, who inspire me daily and motivate me to be better. Always know how much love and confidence I have in both of you, so very proud to be your Dad.

My siblings, brother Steve and sister Susie, who provide unconditional love, and my late parents Bob and Joan Nabors. They were (and are) the best support system a son could ask for. I miss them dearly, but feel their presence daily.

SPECIAL
ACKNOWLEDGEMENT

The majority of the interviews in this book with myself and Drew Brees initially aired on Cox Sports Television. CST signed Brees to an exclusive contract for 14 seasons before the 2007 season through the 2020 campaign. The CST interviews included one-on-ones after each Saints game and several from our yearly in-studio segments. These segments were broadcast on CST's weekly shows, "Saints Gameday," and "Saints Tonight."

TABLE OF
CONTENTS

Foreword: Doug Flutie. i

Introduction: *(A Wedding, A Sharpie & Vintage Brees)* .1

Chapter 1: Legacy *(The Brees Generation)*. 11

Chapter 2: The Ultimate Competitor 31

Chapter 3: Defying The Critics 45

Chapter 4: The Payton Factor/Game Planning. 55

Chapter 5: Spinning Records 79

Chapter 6: Family Life 101

Chapter 7: Behind The Scenes 117

Chapter 8: Extending His Prime 135

Chapter 9: Retirement: Broadcasting Brees & Beyond? 143

Acknowledgments 159

About the Author. 161

FOREWORD
BY **DOUG FLUTIE**

When I first met Drew Brees, he wasn't a future Hall of Famer. He was a 22-year-old second-round pick for the San Diego Chargers out of Purdue. I would later tell him, "When you become a starter, never let your backup see the field." Ironically, I was his backup. Our situation was vastly different than the heated competition I had previously experienced during my days in Buffalo with Rob Johnson. The reason it was different was that I knew my place in San Diego. Drew was the high draft pick. He was gonna be the guy, and it was my job to groom him. I was just the placeholder for the moment.

It helped that we got along great because when I look back on those years, I would say that part of the reason I love Drew so much, and pulled for him, was because nothing was handed to him. He may have been a high draft choice and was the heir apparent for my job, but he had to battle for the spot. He struggled at first and had it taken away but kept working and, because of that, really started seeing the results. I appreciated the fact Drew always had to grind. Once he made it to San Diego, he suffered his shoulder injury, so he continually had to work hard and prove himself, which I respected greatly.

I really connect with guys like Drew because I can identify with him. Like Drew, I had a chip on my shoulder about the six-foot-four guy who walks in, is anointed the starter by his team, proceeds to struggle, yet gets chance after chance. That drives me nuts! Drew was hardly that guy. He was the guy who had to bust his tail every step of the way. Drew and I had similar obstacles with our height. We continually had to answer questions about it, but I appreciated that, being a smaller quarterback, he never used his height as an excuse. In his early years, at the age of 22 or 23, would I have predicted that Drew would become a Hall of Famer one day? I couldn't say that, but I did think he'd be successful.

When Drew went to New Orleans, I was surprised his career took off the way it did, with him breaking records and becoming one of the best quarterbacks of all time. Yet I never ruled that type of stuff out for him. What separated him from the pack was his ability to squeeze the most out of his talent. To become a successful NFL quarterback, you need to work and have the right skills to play the position. Drew possessed those. He was determined, and that's what made the difference.

After playing with him in San Diego, I thought Drew would be good. My expectation was that Drew would go to a couple of Pro Bowls, do well and become a successful starter. But to take his game to where he did in New Orleans was a combination of hard work, being in the right offense with the right people around him and having the right coach. Drew took full advantage.

In my mind, beyond his amazing accuracy and outstanding completion rate, what Drew will most be remembered for is going to New Orleans, reviving a city at a crucial time in its history, and winning a Super Bowl. He was the right guy to lead the way.

I was able to watch Drew lead the Saints to their first world championship in person. In the first half of the game in South Florida, I was sitting in a box with the Patriots. But the whole game, I had been texting with his wife, Brittany. Our families remained close after all those years. She was a nervous wreck in the second half and invited me to come to the Brees family box. As we saw Saints cornerback Tracy Porter intercept Peyton Manning and run the ball back for a touchdown to seal the deal, I thought to myself, "Oh my God, Drew is winning his Super Bowl." I remember getting a big hug from Brittany and feeling so excited for her and my old teammate.

I sincerely felt a sense of pride because I had spent a lot of time with Drew up until that point. I don't try to take credit for anything he's done, yet I'm flattered hearing him say nice things about our relationship and the impact it's had on him over the years. So often, you don't realize the influence you're having on someone when you're working together. You never truly know how your words or actions connect with them. But I'm proud to have been a part of Drew's journey. And what a great journey it's been.

Doug Flutie is a Heisman Trophy winner who played 21 professional seasons of football spanning three decades, including four seasons as a teammate of Drew Brees with the San Diego Chargers.

INTRODUCTION
(A WEDDING, A SHARPIE & VINTAGE BREES)

Many have asked me this question: "Is Drew Brees as nice as he seems?" Instead of providing a stock clichéd answer, I always respond by telling my go-to story because it says it all about one of the best quarterbacks in NFL history.

Over the years, we've had fun putting his eventual broadcasting and adlib skills to work. On many occasions, he provided me random cameo performances in a few videos I've sent to friends and co-workers. One that stood out was back in 2008, after a Saints win, I told Drew that a good friend of mine was getting married but noted that I had to work and wouldn't be able to make the wedding. So, I asked if he would assist me with a fun video message? Drew didn't hesitate and seemed to like being a part of the fun.

Without briefing him, we went right into an impromptu skit, where I looked into the camera and said, "John and Katharine, I'm sorry I can't make your wedding, but at least I was invited. I have a friend who is kind of hurt he wasn't?"

At that moment, Drew walked into the shot and said, "John, I know the mail in New Orleans sometimes gets lost, but not a card or anything?" We keep it going as I say, "Drew, it's too bad because I hear you give great wedding gifts?" Drew immediately goes into full actor mode, looks into the camera, fakes like he's about to cry, and says, "Yes, I do, but I guess you'll never know," and walks out of the shot looking hurt while simultaneously wiping the fake tears out of his eyes.

If that wasn't enough, the best part came after we turned the camera off. I thought Drew had left, but he came back and asked me, "Was that ok?"

This story answers not only the many "What's Drew Brees like?" questions I get, but it also depicts how he approaches everything in his life. He's the ultimate perfectionist, whether it's the Saints weekly game plan or my goofy tribute to an old friend. He always gives his best effort, whether it's a charitable request or his quest to complete every pass in every game. And that is genuinely how he has lived his life.

Drew Brees never does anything halfway. He understands the platform he has and the responsibility that goes with it.

His self-awareness, whether it's routinely signing every autograph after a training camp practice or squeezing every ounce of his athletic ability (more so perhaps than any other player in NFL history) is why he is the real deal in all areas of his life.

My relationship with Drew started unexpectedly but took off in a rather remarkable fashion. It was 2007, and he had just finished his first season with the Saints. He was at Walt Disney World for a marketing shoot but was also in the process of recovering from a dislocated left elbow injury he had suffered in the Pro Bowl. Though I covered Drew's first season in New Orleans, I had never interviewed him one-on-one until that day. Me and my crew and another from ESPN were the only ones there, and after our interview, I overheard Drew tell one of the ESPN producers, "If you ever need to contact me, call my marketing agent Chris Stuart." I didn't have a notepad on me, but my videographer had a sharpie. I quickly eavesdropped, wrote Stuart's number on my hand, and later put it on paper. It was one of the best moves of my career.

You see, later that week, I called Stuart while I was in San Diego shooting a documentary on Saints rookie running back Reggie Bush. At the time, I was hoping Stuart would sign off on a similar project with Brees. Stuart just happens to be based in San Diego and, as he is prone to do over the years, promptly got back to me with great news. Stuart said the documentary idea was good but upped the ante. He said he had brought some of the athletes he represents with cable networks similar to the one I worked for at Cox Sports Television (CST) in New Orleans. Since he had brokered great deals where his clients have teamed up with these networks on many fun projects such as reviewing movies with their wives, Stuart wondered if I would be interested in making a similar deal with Brees and CST? I almost dropped my cellphone!

The sharpie supplied phone number and the subsequent phone conversation with Stuart turned into an unbelievable run for me, CST, and Drew Brees. The result was a 14-year partnership with Cox Sports Television, where I was privileged to host an exclusive postgame interview with Drew after every preseason, regular season, and postseason game from 2007 to his final career-ending game in the 2020-21 playoffs. We also conducted a "State of the Brees" in-studio interview each season. In all, we did an unprecedented 275 one-on-one interviews together. This book captures the best of those interviews, plus a tremendous complementary perspective from those who played, followed, and worked with Drew.

This book aims to provide a unique look into the makeup and motivation of his 15-year career in New Orleans.

We delve into the specific thought process around his longevity, competitiveness, relationship with Sean Payton, and love for his family. In addition, I highlight some of his best games, how he plans to attack his future after football, and I reflect on his immense legacy in nine chapters for the Saints' No. 9.

By interviewing Drew on so many occasions, I was able to pick up on his lingo. As the team leader, he would frequently use similar fallback phrases to summarize both his and the Saints' mindset attacking a game, a practice, or any moment of adversity. One of his favorites was "time on task," which described how he approached his football life. All of his teammates will say they could never beat him to the building and never saw him leave before them at the end of the day. Drew's time on task mantra meant getting the most out of his film work, his extra work with his receivers and he carried it over into every aspect of his life, including, most importantly, his time with his growing family.

Drew often was a better interview after a loss than a win, and even in good times he would always find something about his game or the offense that needed to be improved on. His favorite lines were repeatedly characterizing the Saints as "an ascending team," meaning they were headed in the right direction but weren't where he wanted them to be. Whether it was the first win of a season or a much-needed victory after a losing streak, Drew would often say we "broke the seal," meaning it was a good day at the office, but he'd always add that more "time on task" was needed, both for him and the football team.

The proof of the Saints quarterback being a better interview after a loss was evident in how our segments went after arguably his two most brutal defeats as a Saint. Following the infamous "no-call" NFC Championship game against the Rams in 2019, the one in which game officials failed to call what replays showed to be a blatant pass interference penalty against Saints wide receiver Tommylee Lewis. That non-call played a significant part in preventing New Orleans from reaching the Super Bowl that year, but Drew, knowing his body language was essential both on the field and off when facing the media, refused to make excuses and never became overly emotional. His responses had to illustrate his role as the leader of the team.

It's often hard to get perspective from athletes after a crushing loss, but Drew impressively and effortlessly answered all of my post Rams questions. When I asked him if such a heart-breaking loss made it difficult to appreciate all the great things that he and the Saints had done that season, he replied: "This is all a tough pill to swallow, but let me say this too about the call: At the end of the day, we as players only can worry about the things we control, and a lot of that stuff is out of our control. Play the game to the best of our ability, play the game with fundamentals and technique and sometimes things go your way. And sometimes they don't. But at the end of the day, you just have to move on to the next play. So, to me, there was no lingering effect from that. Once the call is made or not made, it's over. Let's move on."

These comments were uttered less than 30 minutes after a devasting loss, but they exemplify how Drew knew his role and was aware that he needed to be positive as the team leader. It's something he did over and over throughout his career, and it trickled down to his teammates and it's a big reason why the Saints became one of the most consistently successful teams in the NFL while Drew was leading the way. On that somber day in New Orleans after the NFC Championship loss to the Rams, Drew sent a message to his many fans too, saying, "This was a special year, it was a great year, and I hope the fans feel that way too because they were a special part of it. They were incredible today. They were incredible all season. You know, that's part of what hurt so much, too. You wanted it for them (adding more emphasis). You want it for them."

Drew loved winning as much as anybody, but his leadership after losses consistently stood out.

For example, on January 14th, 2018 in the 2017-18 playoffs, the Vikings led the Saints 17-0 at the half, but Drew brought the Saints back by engineering an impressive second-half comeback on the road in Minnesota's brand-new U.S. Bank Stadium. His pinpoint touchdown pass to Saints running back Alvin Kamara with just over three minutes remaining in the game gave the Saints its first lead, and when Saints kicker Wil Lutz kicked a field goal that put New Orleans up 24-23 with 25 seconds left, it seemed like the Saints would win. But they didn't. In pulling off what became known as the "Minneapolis Miracle," Vikings quarterback Case Keenum found receiver Stefon Diggs.

What happened next would tear the heart out of the Saints and its fanbase for months. Rookie Saints safety Marcus Williams had the perfect position to make the play on Diggs but inexplicably whiffed on the tackle. Diggs did the rest. An improbable 61-yard game-winning touchdown. It was the first time in NFL playoff history a touchdown was scored with time expiring. The first of several painful daggers for the Saints in the latter stages of Drew's career in the postseason, but in this instance, just as he did during all of the other moments of heartache, Drew lead with his actions and his words.

During our one-on-one outside the locker room, he told me "I love this team. I love being a part of this team. This is a team that loves one another, cares about one another, loves playing football, knows how to have fun, knows how to work. It's the most fun I've had playing football in a long time."

Drew's demeanor after losses was admirable, but in 14 years of doing interviews after the highest of highs and the lowest of lows, he amazingly never lost his cool, not once. When we first worked together, he frequently finished the interview by walking behind the camera as I was wrapping up, giving me a thumbs up to make sure we were good until I gave him the heads up. In those days, he didn't have any kids, so in subsequent years, as his family grew from one to four children, his time understandably became more and more precious after games. Thus, the thumbs-up behind the camera turned into more time on his cell phone back home to check in on his family.

Through it all, Drew always delivered and took these postgame chats as seriously as he did everything in his football sphere. However, one interview specifically stood out, because it summarized what Drew consistently gave us. This interview personifies the content in the book as it displays the full Brees platter: his competitive side, his leadership, his drive, even his family.

It was a postgame interview after he and the Saints beat the Arizona Cardinals during the 2019 season. It was Drew's first game back after missing five weeks with a thumb injury. Many (including me) thought that with the bye week coming up next, he should have skipped this game and come back two weeks later. That would have given him six weeks instead of five to recover from his injury. But to that the then-41-year-old Saints quarterback offered an excellent counter argument.

I asked him after the game, "Drew, there was a faction out there who said, "C'mon, just rest this game. You have the bye week coming up. Did you understand that line of thinking from some of the fans out there?" Drew's response tells you everything you need to know about how he approached football, especially later in his career. Laughing, he paused for a moment to collect his thoughts, then said, "Listen, I'm on borrowed time. I never thought I'd be playing this long, right? I'm gonna take advantage of every single moment, every single opportunity I get. If I can play, I want to be with my teammates. I want to play for them."

This moment illustrates what made Drew so unique. With seemingly nothing more to prove, he constantly had to prove something to himself while he made it a priority to soak in every second of football because he loved the game so much. What made him great was this appreciation, along with his ultimate competitive streak, even when it came to rebounding from a thumb injury. When I asked him when he knew he would play that game, he pointed to his head and said, "The Saturday before last week - up, hear I did. I just had to convince Coach Payton. I don't want to miss games. I'm not programmed to miss games." Drew had specific timetables regarding this injury, but he was determined to beat them all. "I think the initial prognosis from everybody (moving his hands like he would push away his doubters) but um (pauses smiles, laughs) I wasn't gonna take that (laughing). I'm not gonna be reckless about it, that wouldn't have been fair to my team."

This interview personified Drew in the many postgame one-on-one's we shared. He may be a private man in many ways, but he consistently displayed his passion for the game. "The quarterback position is about being efficient, positive plays, getting yourself in good situations, getting out of bad situations, minimizing losses. You are kind of a crisis manager at times, and then (he makes a fist and hits his hand) when you have the opportunity to make the play, you make the play."

Spot on perspective, a rare competitive fire, and the constant mindset of proving people wrong. It was a vintage Brees interview from our 14 years together where I closed the session by asking him if his three sons and youngest child, daughter Rylen, would have to go easy on Dad during the upcoming bye week? "That's right, they're rough," Brees said. "Rylen Brees is rough. She's the roughest because she just jumps on you without telling you."

This postgame interview had it all and perfectly summarizes what you will collect from this book.

The sum of all the parts made Drew a legend for life in New Orleans and a future Hall of Famer, let us count the ways.

1

Legacy

(THE BREES GENERATION)

It's hard to quantify the legacy of Drew Brees because there are many layers. He was more than just a football player to Saints fans in Louisiana and the neighboring Gulf Coast. The timing of his arrival and eventual impact couldn't have been better as the region was devasted and nearly destroyed by Hurricane Katrina. Before Katrina, the Saints had been hurting for decades, too, but for different reasons. The "Who Dats," as Saints fans are famously known, comprise one of the most loyal fan bases in the NFL, but they didn't feel the love in return for the majority of their existence.

Fans of the black and gold had been yearning for a leader for decades, so it was ironic that a quarterback recovering from a career-threatening shoulder injury would be the perfect candidate to instantly provide relief to a city and fanbase in such dire need. The new franchise signal-caller immediately delivered both on and off the field, whether it was picking up a hammer to re-build the community's ravaged infrastructure, raising millions of dollars for a multitude of projects through his Dream Foundation,or simultaneously lifting the spirits of his team on the field in a way that greatly surpassed anyone's wildest expectations.

Drew grew up in nearby Austin, Texas, but his first trip to New Orleans didn't occur until he was 23. "It was for my college roommate's wedding (in the summer of 2003), so it was Bourbon Street, that New Orleans experience, which is fun, but it was very limited until 2006."

During his inaugural trip to the Crescent City as a tourist and member of the San Diego Chargers, the young quarterback had no reason to believe that a few years later, he would change the landscape of not only the city's football team but the region.

"It exceeded my wildest dreams and expectations," Drew told me, reflecting on his career after retirement. "I really had no idea what to expect when I first got to New Orleans because I had very limited exposure, and it was at a point in my career (coming off shoulder surgery) when I had my own inner doubts (whether) I (would) come back and play at a high level."

For Drew, it was love at first sight. He instantly felt a connection with the city. "I think the thing that struck me more than anything when I first came to New Orleans was everywhere I went, every fan I bumped into on the street, said to me, 'Thank you for considering to be a part of this city and this community.' It was nothing about the Saints, it was nothing about football, it was just, 'Thank you for being a part of this city.'"

It was a special feeling he absorbed and appreciated immediately. "So that struck me, that is a bit unusual. Obviously, there is something to this community, the fabric of this community, the way they see themselves, their level of appreciation for me just wanting to come down and give it a consideration, that really stuck out."

Before Drew arrived in New Orleans, the Saints had enjoyed just seven winning seasons in 39 years. Before Drew, the Saints had recorded just one playoff win. When Drew retired, ironically number 9, left behind nine winning seasons and nine playoff wins. ESPN stats noted that before his arrival, the Saints had a .403 winning percentage which was tied with the

Cardinals for the third-worst in the NFL. By contrast, from 2006 to when Drew retired after the 2020 season, the Saints had a .625 winning clip, which was fourth-best in the league. You can debate the best quarterbacks in NFL history, but none reversed the fortunes of a franchise the way this Saints quarterback transformed New Orleans.

His contributions immediately impacted the Saints, yet arguably the best indication of the legacy of Drew Brees is seen in his generational effect. While many generations witnessed Saints fans wearing bags over their heads to hide their faces and suffered through seemingly endless strings of heartache and heartbreak, Drew's arrival changed the culture and altered the mindset as the "Brees generation" developed new hope. This optimism included yearly expectations of division titles, playoff games, and Super Bowl talk: a far cry from what their predecessors had experienced.

For perspective, if you were born in the 21st century, you were at worst six years old when Drew started in New Orleans, so all you remember is Saints success. On the other hand, if you were 25 years old or under when he retired, your membership in the Brees generation enabled you never to experience the tough days of being heartbroken by your hometown football team in the ways your parents or grandparents had. This generational shift went from the many who endured endless losing seasons to those who enjoyed several playoff appearances.

It was the Brees effect.

For reference, you have the Romig family, who presents the perfect barometer of the history of the Saints fanbase before and after Drew Brees. The Romigs not only boast three generations of New Orleans bloodlines, but several family members have been around the organization since its inception. The patriarch of the family, Jerry Romig, was the team's public address announcer for 44 seasons, calling an unprecedented 446 straight games beginning in 1969. Due to a myriad of health issues, Jerry had to step down from his position after the 2013 season. However, the job stayed in the family as son Mark, who sounded almost exactly like his father, was the replacement. It was a comforting transition for Saints fans.

Mark Romig is assisted in the booth by sister Mary Beth who spots for him. And then you have brother Jay Romig, who like his father before him, is a member of the Saints Hall of Fame, Jay earning his place for his work as the team's administrative director. You can ask anyone inside the Saints building and they will tell you Jay Romig does everything behind the scenes. He is the man that many within the walls of the organization affectionately call "Jay Bird," a name given to him when he started in the late seventies by then Saints coach Hank Stram. Jay Bird is the glue that holds it all together for the Saints, from travel arrangements to postgame meals and everything in between. Jay and the Romig family have collectively witnessed the Saints' entire roller coaster ride from its humble beginnings in the sixties to its heyday in the Brees and Payton era.

Mary Beth Romig summed up what life was like for Saints fans before Brees. Especially in those early years, she explained, fans of the black and gold tried to stay optimistic, always looking for a silver lining, no matter how thin it would be some Sundays. "It must be like golf," she said. "You have that great shot that keeps you coming back to play another round. There was something about the Saints all those seasons."

Like many others in New Orleans, this family has an appreciation of what Drew Brees brought not only to the Saints but to a city ravaged by Hurricane Katrina as the Romigs lost three homes to the natural disaster. For them, Brees' immediate impact on and off the field lifted the spirits for everyone in the area. "It was a curtain opening," said Janice Romig, the wife of Jerry and the woman this family affectionally calls "Honey." Mary Beth says Brees' presence delivered "joy and rapture, tremendous emotion. When we leave a game and Mark and I are walking down the concourse with fans, everybody is so excited and hopeful."

That attitude represents a stark contrast from previous years for the black and gold faithful. While the Saints enjoyed a great run of playoff appearances under head coach Jim Mora and secured the franchise's first playoff win under Jim Haslett, it was mostly a collection of sad Saints Sundays before Drew Brees changed everything. "People in the city wanted to believe in them and they did, but it was (tough) when some started to wear the bags on their heads," said Janice.

The Romig rule was a strict mandate: no family member could don a bag over their head, but they too felt the frustration expressed for years by so many others in the fanbase. Janice Romig couldn't leave the games early as she was with her husband working on the public address duties. "I used to kid Mom. She was with Dad, so she was (using air quotes) stuck at the games," Mark Romig remembered. Janice replied, "I was there till the last play."

Her kids had other options during the lean years and often took advantage. "We didn't have to (stay till the end). We could leave in the third quarter or earlier if necessary," said Mark, who often did when he was in his 30s. "I would get up at halftime and think, 'Let's beat the traffic. It's not worth it,' so we would leave. It just jarred Mom big time, but she was good and didn't say much about it."

For Mark, this mindset would change with the arrival of Brees and the opportunity he would ultimately have in replacing his father. "When Dad retired and the Saints asked me to kind of sit in his chair, I called Mom and said, 'I get to be the announcer now.' She told me, 'But you have to stay for the whole game now.'"

Drew gave Saints fans a reason to stay as he changed both the hopes of the Who Dat Nation and the mindset within the organization. Behind the scenes, Jay Romig saw the legacy Drew built internally with the Saints.

"He's just the ultimate professional," Jay said. "He'll always find time before a game when we get to the hotel possibly to sign a few autographs and after the game, he is so deliberate about what he does as a professional, it spread throughout the whole organization."

Jay Romig has countless Brees stories of the Saints quarterback going the extra mile for fans, such as the time the team was in New Jersey and a police officer, who was a part of the escort unit for the Saints, asked if he and his son could meet Drew? "The policeman begged me, is there any way I can meet Drew?" Jay Romig remembers. "When we got to the hotel, he met with him in a separate room for a few minutes. I still hear from him, it was a little thing Drew did, but it made somebody's life forever."

While many of the Romigs survived the tough beginnings and sometimes excruciating subsequent decades of heartbreak and heartache of Saints football, the third generation basked in the Brees generation: chock full of playoff contention, including the franchise's first Super Bowl title. It's an exciting dynamic for an NFL franchise to have mainly losing football for decades, then see it followed up by years of consistent relevance.

Blake Romig was born in 1995, so all he can remember are the good years. He has no recollection of the nightmare of bags over fans' heads or the inexplicable personnel moves, such as trading all of its draft picks in the 1999 NFL Draft for Texas Heisman Trophy running back Ricky Williams, that crippled the franchise for years. He's part of the generation of Saints fans who only know success, in larger part to a quarterback who arrived in 2006 when Blake was 11 years old.

Blake's first actual memory of a Saints game in the Superdome was Brees' first, when the team returned after being away for a season due to Hurricane Katrina. Blake remembers the emotion of the Saints' monumental Monday Night win versus the Falcons. "I went to some games before that, but the one where I started to remember was that one." It was quite an introduction to

Saints football as it was arguably the most memorable home game in franchise history. It began with the legendary blocked punt from Saints' special teamer Steve Gleason, which led to the tone setting opening score and featured the iconic halftime show with U2 and Green Day.

However, the highlight was an appropriate song that hits home with many New Orleans fans, especially those who comprise the Brees generation. Originally written by the Skids, a Scottish punk band, it was the signature song in the halftime show. "The Saints are coming. That's one of my favorite songs," Blake said. When I mentioned the term "Brees generation," he responded the way so many of his peers would, "Oh, yeah."

Drew's imprint will forever leave a generation of fans with an entirely different mindset of what Saints football is all about. For that Blake Romig feels fortunate. He knows what his father and grandfather had to experience.

"It's crazy to think about it, but I've never seen a team with fans wearing bags over their heads and stuff like that. I've never even pictured that." For the fans who have only seen Brees set records and keep the Saints relevant, it's hard to complain when he's around the rest of the family who've seen much tougher times. When the third generation Romig hears those stories of the tough Saints years, it makes him appreciate what he's gotten to experience watching the entire career of New Orleans' number 9. "Oh yeah, it does. I mean, the Saints record in the three toughest seasons I experienced was 7-9, and I thought the world was ending. But my (family) talks about 3-13 and one-win seasons, things like that. Here I was, struggling on 7-9 and thinking at the time that it can't get worse than this, can it?"

Blake Romig has enjoyed this era as a fan and for years as a part of the team's equipment staff, an experience that has given him a unique look at how much the Saints organization has changed in the 15 years Brees was a member of the organization. It's something many of his peers sometimes take for granted. "I talk about it with my friends a lot because my friends will nit-pick on games. The Saints may end the season with a 12-4 record, but they'll say, 'Man, terrible season.' I say 'What? They won the NFC South. Don't say terrible because it was worse back then. Stick with us. It's 12-4, it's perfect.'"

Drew raised the expectation level for a generation of fans who don't know of the dark years. They only expect an annual run at a Super Bowl. Blake Romig smiles when recalling several discussions he's had with friends surrounding yearly expectations. "We'll talk about how they lost in the first round of the playoffs and I'll say, 'Well at least we made the playoffs.' Sometimes you gotta be happy with that because there were a bunch of years (back in the day) with no playoffs."

The Brees generation may not fully appreciate what Drew did because that's all they've known. But it seems all members of this new era value what he's done for New Orleans. "He changed the city 'cause he and (Coach Sean) Payton came in right after Katrina. Football kind of brought it back together, so he's always great for the city," Blake Romig said. "And as for what he's done for the game, in my opinion, he's the greatest quarterback ever, no question. That can be debated. But what he's done stat-wise is unreal, and his attention to detail is unreal. His work ethic is great. I've never seen anything like that."

Drew changed the culture, the expectations. Like Archie Manning for years before him, he is now synonymous with the Saints moving forward. So, when you think of the Saints, you think of Drew Brees, an honor he appreciates.

"First of all, it's very humbling," he told me when I asked him about his Saints legacy in 2015. "There is a ton of great players who have played for the New Orleans Saints, and I know the organization doesn't necessarily have that reputation as being this consistent winner through the '60s, 70's, 80's and 90's, yet there are some great players for this organization."

More complicated than measuring the impact of Brees in New Orleans is getting Drew to talk about himself. While being aware of his influence, he still appreciated the history of the Saints seemingly daily. "What's cool for me is literally every day as I walk down the hallways of the organization, I see the pictures up on the wall of all of these players, these men. I don't want to start naming them because I know I might miss a few. I don't want to hurt anybody's feelings, but there have been a ton of great ones, and I've had the chance to play with a few of them, which makes it even better."

While Drew respects those that came before him, he's proud of the legacy he helped build. It aimed to transform the fortunes of how the franchise was perceived internally and around the league. "I feel there is a level of respect that our organization has now that maybe it didn't ten years ago," Drew told me in 2015. "We have some of these great players that we can look back on and admire for their accomplishments prior to us all getting here, but I think the teams we've had here since 2006 maybe have kind of been able to make our mark a little bit in the way the New Orleans Saints are perceived around the league."

Drew appreciates that his legacy would be associated with leaving the Saints in a better place than when he entered New Orleans. "I think for anybody, whenever you enter your job, your venture, your passion, you hope that people will look back after it's all said and done and say those guys made it better than when they found it," he said. "I'd like to think that when it's all said and done for us, people will look back and say that stretch really established the Saints as a team that people looked at and admired and respected and (smiling) brought some excitement to."

The impact of his leadership was felt immediately by his teammates. "The first time Drew stood up in front of our team, I didn't know much about Drew Brees until he stood up in our meeting and he talked," former Saints linebacker Scott Shanle said. "When you're in a group of grown men ages 21 to 35 or 36, and the man stands up and starts to talk, and the entire room shuts up, nobody says a thing you have your leader. And so, from that moment when Drew stood up and spoke to us, anything he said was heard throughout the room. That's when you knew you had a franchise quarterback, and you knew you had a guy that was going to take you to the promised land."

Gameday was another aspect of Brees' legacy that his teammates and fans will always appreciate. Traditionally quarterbacks aren't the players leading pregame chants. This responsibility often goes to boisterous defensive stars like former Baltimore Ravens Hall of Fame linebacker Ray Lewis who was known for a myriad of grand entrances during his career. In contrast, Drew, who carefully chooses his words, wanted to take his role as leader to a new level by gathering his teammates before each game in the end zone with a chant, which would truly set the tone. In 2018 we touched on the importance of his pre-game chant, which had become one of his signature staples. I asked him, "Are there times when it's hard to develop a new one and what goes into it?"

"I put a lot into that," Drew told me. " We evolved, going back to 2008 is when we first started doing it. That one was based on the movie "300," right? This is Sparta, this is New Orleans."

The Sparta idea kickstarted a tradition in which Drew enjoyed coming up with new themes each week and each season, collecting ideas from several experiences. "In (2009) the inspiration for that was doing PT (physical training) with the Marines in Guantanamo Bay on of my USO trips. They were barking out cadence as we were running in the middle of the night, and one of them struck me as this would be great for our team. I had to modify it a little bit because they are talking about killing, whereas I needed to talk about winning."

Drew was motivated to make the chants different and fresh, always coming up with the ideas himself while following the lead of his head coach. "That (weekly theme) is established by coach Payton and is added to with leaders on the team or other coaches, yes, but it's definitely a specific theme on what we have to do that week against that team to get a win."

His pregame chants and work ethic will forever be a part of the Brees legacy, as will Drew's penchant to make everyone around him feel at ease. When former Saints wide receiver Marques Colston arrived in New Orleans, he appreciated the fact that despite Drew's cache as the team's starting quarterback and one of the game's elite players, he was so approachable.

"It's weird because as a fan, he's somebody I always looked up to," Colston said. "When I got to (New Orleans), it took a while for me to build up the courage to speak to him. I kind of saw him in a different regard."

Colston quickly discovered a new comfort once he took the field with his new quarterback. "It's funny, but on the field all that stuff goes away. All those emotional things go away. It was in the locker room and just kind of around the building where it was just a little different," Colston said. "When you're being seen in the same light of someone you're a fan of, it's a unique feeling."

Fellow Saints wide receiver Lance Moore concurred as his first year with Brees saw him coming off a season where he was on the practice squad, spent some time playing in Europe, and was still finding his way on the roster. Yet he will never forget the first time he met his new quarterback. Moore was at the Saints training facility early and saw Brees on the other side of the room. At the time, he didn't know how to approach a quarterback who quickly would become a close friend.

"Should I like, go say hello and introduce myself to him? He is going to be my quarterback for this season," Moore said. "Sure enough, as I'm getting my game plan together, he taps my shoulder and says 'Hi, I'm Drew Brees, nice to meet you, let me know if you need anything?' I was kind of like, 'Oh my gosh, this guy came over to me, some guy who he's probably never heard of, practice squad guy the year before, haven't even touched the NFL field yet, and he's asking me if I need anything or, you know, just introducing himself to me."

Moore would catch 38 touchdown passes from Brees, the third most of any Saints target, in his 15 seasons. Yet, the introduction between the two is something Moore will always cherish. "That went a long-ways, as far as in my mind the connection that we formed and built over the next several years," Moore said. "Man, just a blessing that he helped break the ice the way that he did."

Moore's immense respect carried over to everything, even the nickname he had acquired from his teammates that he wasn't fond of, Lance Romance. "There are very few people that I would allow to call me that," Moore said. "(Brees) can get away with a lot. I allowed him to call me Lance Romance. With most other people, (I say), 'Don't call me that, just call me Lance.'"

When I reminded Drew of the nickname and his exclusive rights, he smiled and laughed while appreciating the respect one of his favorite receivers gave him, "It's an honor to know that's my special nickname. It's how you say it too (lowering his voice), it's Lance Romance. You gotta add a little something."

Drew had the ultimate respect of his teammates, but he didn't always enjoy the same recognition outside the Saints' locker room. Despite winning division titles and setting records, amazingly, he was never the MVP of the league. It's a noticeable hole in his resume.

I asked him in 2018 if that bothered him? "I'd rather win a Super Bowl," he quickly replied. "(Being named MVP) is an unbelievable honor. It's a tremendous honor. It's an acknowledgement, it's respect from others that know football and appreciate football and have seen a lot of football, but it's not the end all be all. I just want to win. I know if I take care of that, the other stuff will take care of itself."

The hardest part of interviewing Drew is getting him to talk about himself. While he takes pride in winning, he often deflects to his coach and his teammates. But, during one interview session, I tried to get him to weigh in on how he ranks among his peers?

It was 2018, when upstarts like Patrick Mahomes and Deshaun Watson were gaining on the old guard such as Brees, Tom Brady, and Aaron Rodgers. I wanted to know Drew's perception of where he stood among the game's elite signal-callers? Despite all of his accomplishments, the consensus was Drew remained underappreciated. On this matter, the ultra-competitive Saints quarterback preferred not to engage.

"I don't think too much of it," Drew told me. "As long as I have the respect of my teammates and they know I'm going to battle for them every Sunday and throughout the week and that I'm representing them the best that I can, I can't control what others say or don't say."

Knowing Drew's competitive nature, I followed up by asking if it lights a fire in him when he hears pundits say Brady, Rodgers, and Brees, in that order? With a smile, Drew replied, "Those guys are more talented throwing the ball than me." I was surprised by the candid response and said, "Really?" Drew continued, "Yeah they're more talented throwing the ball than me."

When I asked him if that motivated him, his demeanor noticeably changed. Suddenly, I saw the competitor come out a little more. "Trust me, I'm always motivated, I always have a chip on my shoulder, always have something to prove, but it doesn't matter who the names are in front or back. Everybody has to have something to talk about. I have nothing but respect for those guys. Those guys do it the right way, and they've done it at a high level for a very long time."

Drew respects his peers and their talents, knowing they push him to be better but at the same time, he appreciates those in the league who are able to perform at a high level over many years. "I love watching film on those two (Brady and Rodgers), and others. I look forward to pulling up their game tape each week, especially if we're playing similar opponents."

While the quarterback debates will rage on, Drew's legacy is cemented in New Orleans. A resume' built on reshaping a perception of a franchise and kickstarting its fanbase. It's a legacy rooted in leadership, an inspired work ethic that translated to making all of his teammates better. Many will debate where Drew ranks among the all-time greats, but he believes it's an honor merely to be in the conversation.

"It absolutely is. It's very humbling," Drew told me in 2018. "I don't want to be a part of that discussion. I don't have an opinion. I'm just gonna go about my job to the best of my ability, and we'll let everything speak for itself."

The Saints quarterback is hesitant to sing his own praises, but there are countless stories of teammates who offered up plenty of emotion. It could be teammates who played with Drew for years or, in the case of backup quarterback Jameis Winston, only one season. Winston arrived in New Orleans in 2020, after a tumultuous five-year run as the starter for the Tampa Bay Buccaneers. During that time, Winston's work ethic was never questioned, but his decision-making was. Ironically, the last game Brees and Winston played together was against the Bucs in the playoffs. At the end of this Saints loss, the cameras caught a shot of Drew delivering Winston a seemingly inspired message.

Months later, Winston reflected on the moment. It was a sincere and emotional response at the end of a press conference devoted to the news he was re-signing with the Saints. Throughout the entire presser, Winston had been smiling and upbeat until the end. Then he was asked about his final exchange with Drew and its impact? Winston's mood changed instantly. He became emotional to the point where he choked up and had to pause for a moment as he reflected on his lone season with his Saints mentor.

"Being able to have an entire season with Drew Brees (pausing) was a dream of mine," he said for him to put his arm around me and (offer) any encouraging words after I saw the resilience, the passion (pauses, chokes up) the way he approached every single day for that to even be a story, I was touched. I'm speechless, that really gets me emotional because I really love Drew Brees. I don't think he understands or knows how much he means to me and my family for real."

Winston's actions personified how Drew could impact a teammate, even if it's only over the course of one season. For Saints offensive lineman Zach Strief, the impact was made over several seasons. Strief's body of work with his former quarterback was far more extensive, and so were his emotions at his retirement presser following the 2017 season. The 6-foot 7-inch former right tackle was known for his smarts and wit, yet he didn't have a reputation for being overly emotional. That all changed at the point in the press conference when he started talking about what it meant to play with Drew. Uncharacteristically, Strief cried at the podium. He repeatedly had to stop and collect himself when talking about the man he shared a huddle with for his entire career.

"For the past eight years, I played in front of the most prolific passer in NFL history," Strief said fighting back and eventually giving way to tears. "Drew Brees has been the single greatest motivation for me as a player."

For Strief, watching Brees work up close changed his career. "Every day, I would walk into the building and pass Drew watching him," said Strief at his retirement presser with Brees in attendance. "My greatest drive as a player was not to let you down (long pause to gather himself). You're the greatest leader I've ever been around, and I admire you so much as a player but more as a person. Being a small part of your Hall of Fame career has been my greatest honor as a player (tearing up). I will miss being around you on a daily basis. Thank you for everything you've done and continue to do."

Strief told me former Saints running back Deuce McAllister's best advice going into that press conference was not to cry, but he couldn't hold himself back. Strief, like so many of Brees' teammates, whether their tenure was brief like Winston's or lengthy, they all felt a keen sense of loyalty and respect for a player who showed them how to be a professional.

For Strief, the tears for Brees that day originated from him remembering how he never got to personally thank his college coach, Northwestern University's Randy Walker, for all that he had done for hm. Walker passed away in June of 2006, right after Strief was drafted. Regrettably, Strief missed the chance to thank Walker in person for what he had meant to him. He didn't want to have the same regrets with his longtime quarterback.

"I never got to share and acknowledge what a big impact (Walker) had on me, (so) when I went into that press conference for Drew, that was in the back of my head the whole time," Strief explained. "You know, don't miss the opportunity to really share with these guys what you feel about them and about the impact they've had."

Strief seized the moment, saving the biggest tribute of his goodbye for Drew. "All that preparation, all that time that (Brees) invested and his kind of relentlessness and consistency in preparation, I always felt (like that) elongated my career a good bit and that without him, it wouldn't have worked out the way that it did. I felt it was important to share that."

The sharing was necessary, but the emotional outburst from the biggest man on the Saints roster was natural and unexpected. "It was just the opportunity, it was kind of like a realization," Strief said. "I'm already here, I'm already crying, so I might as well get it all out. I think most people that knew me were surprised, and the amount of emotion that was in it, but it all stems back from this reality that I never got to tell someone who meant a whole lot to me that they meant a lot to me. I didn't want to make that mistake again."

Strief was one of the best interviews of the Sean Payton era. His intellect and eloquence saw him making the unprecedented move of going from the playing field directly into the broadcast booth as the team's play-by-play man for three seasons before eventually moving to Payton's coaching staff. He was the consummate team leader, and his final words as a player spoke for many in the Saints locker room.

"I knew, and I watched how much of a sacrifice, how much of a time commitment (Brees) made to be the player that he was," Strief said. "I'm not saying necessarily that he was doing it for me, but I do think that a lot of it stemmed from his desire to not let his guys down, and that always kind of (resonated) with me. I always felt that same pressure of not wanting to let him down. That was a driving force for me, a kind of big realization to share with someone."

Drew's knack for knowing the pulse of the team was uncanny. It was rare to play for the same group as long as he did with the same coach and a steady stream of the same core teammates for years. When he spoke, his teammates listened.

"I'll never forget before the playoffs started (in 2009), Drew stood up there, and maybe it was something his grandfather said," Scott Shanle remembered. "He said there are three types of people in the world: people who want things to happen, people who wish for things to happen, and people who go out and make it happen. That's something I can tell you I've used with my own kids."

For Shanle, Drew was much more than game-winning drives and gaudy stats. He set the tone for the Saints. "So there's been a lot of things I've admired about Drew from afar," Shanle said. "Most of them I think have come after playing, but the things he did for us in our locker room, we were all beneficiaries of his leadership and his dedication to excellence."

For his teammates, it was an honor to be a part of his legacy, which was bigger than football. "I think it will go beyond football," Lance Moore acknowledged. "He's somebody that brought hope, not just around the organization, but the whole city, the whole Gulf Coast region, the devastation that everybody had to deal with Hurricane Katrina. All the bad years, the Aints and you know, just the positivity that he brought, the hope that he brought, basically transforming that whole region into now thinking and expecting the Saints to win. To do all the things that he was able to do, and

I would say exceed expectations, is nothing short of amazing."

"That stuff is humbling," Drew told me after I shared with him those heartfelt sentiments from his teammates. But, a big part of the Brees legacy is the relationships he fostered inside the huddle and the locker room. "I think a huge part of this game and what I'll miss about this game is the relationships you have in the locker room, the guys that you get to wake up and see every day," he said. "Man, there's those moments you look back and just cherish those memories."

Memories touched his coaches and teammates and served as inspiration for his fanbase, including the Romig family. While Janice, Mark, Jay, and Mary Beth have been fans from the beginning, the family's eleven grandchildren only know winning since Brees arrived in 2006. "Well, the grandchildren, we've talked with them about that before," Janice said. "I've told them all about Dempsey hitting that long field goal at Tulane Stadium (a reference to New Orleans kicker Tom Dempsey's 63-yard game-winning field goal in 1970, which set an NFL record for longest kick). "We were losing and a lot of people had left the game when Jerry (Romig) said, 'It's good! It's good!'"

Among the fans who had lost hope and left early was a member of the Romig family. "My own brother was outside," Janice recalls. "He said I could hear Jerry, why did I leave? We did have hard times but we came through them with a leader like Drew."

For the Romig family and so many others, Brees provided something they'd never had as Saints fans. He reversed the fortunes of an once floundering franchise and brought a new hope of doing something special each week. "The fact you could go to each game and know that Drew was there, it would be ok," Mark Romig said. "It was all right because Drew was there with Coach Payton and the rest of the team."

A newfound hope was instilled in the Superdome for 15 years and absorbed in the control booth where the Romigs were working every home game. "It changed the tenor of the control booth because we were really pumped and excited every game day for whatever was gonna come. We enjoyed it so much more because you had a feeling of hope every game," Mary Beth said.

Hope is what Drew Brees provided his team and city more than arguably any other quarterback in NFL history. He made the Saints and New Orleans believe it could be a winner year in and year out. Brees delivered a new identity, one the Romigs and Saints fans hope will serve as a precedent moving forward.

"That's the lesson we should all take away from this. If you stay focused and work hard and you have a team attitude, you can achieve greatness. There was a degree of excellence, and I think Drew would expect us as a team to surpass that," Mark said. "And it's not gonna change (now) that he's gone, I think it's something that he's instilled in all of us that will stay around forever. It's definitely a difference of what it was, and it is now."

2

The Ultimate Competitor

You could make a case that the two most competitive men on the planet shared a San Diego quarterback room in 2002. I once turned the tables on Drew and asked him who the most competitive guy he's ever been around is? Without hesitation, he said, "Doug Flutie."

Flutie became Drew's mentor after he entered the league as a second-round draft pick of the Chargers. It was a perfect match as the quarterback duo had much in common. For starters, neither looked the part, each failing to meet the prototypical measurements of an NFL quarterback. They were too short to play the position, first in college then the pros. Neither was a five-star recruit or a sure-fire first-round draft pick. As a result, they shared a rare competitive fire. And over time, all of the doubt and criticism mounted and ultimately created gigantic chips on their respective shoulders.

Drew and Flutie were kindred spirits from the start. "We hit it off pretty good," Flutie told me from the dugout of his longtime adult baseball league. Flutie hasn't lost those competitive juices in his retirement. He not only plays baseball but is active in a hockey league, surfs regularly from his home in Melbourne Beach, Florida, and plays drums in a band with his brothers. Like Drew, Flutie can't sit still and lives for any opportunity to create competition. In Drew, Flutie found the perfect teammate/little brother. "We hung out, we talked, we joked, we played games," Flutie said of their relationship.

Drew's post-practice quarterback competitions became legendary with Saints fans and often went viral on social media, but their origin dates back to his early days with Flutie, where they came up with a plethora of ways to compete. These early quarterback battles were eerily similar to the contests Drew would later implement in competing with his Saints backup quarterbacks. "It was a lot of fun because I thought that Drew and I, especially when he was young, were very similar characters," Flutie said.

These two "characters" stoked their competitive fires in many sports. "I remember buying Drew a dozen baseballs and a bat for his birthday and saying, 'C'mon we're going to go hit,'" Flutie recalls. "We went to some high school field and took batting practice and we had a blast. You know, things like that, messing around that's what we did." Flutie's baseball present was delivered at a seemingly formal birthday party that Brittany Brees was throwing for her husband. "Brittany throws it at this fancy place, and there are a few high-profile people at it, with a nice view of the city, and here I am giving him baseballs and a bat and saying, 'Tomorrow morning, we're gonna go hit,'" Flutie recalls with a laugh.

These two big kids would have fun wherever they went. And while the competitions started with baseball, they quickly progressed to the football field, where Drew and Flutie began by just throwing footballs at goalposts. The veteran and the rookie went mano-y-mano during their first year together and later drew first-round rookie quarterback Phillip Rivers into the battle. "Drew, Phillip, and I used to do it all the time, then as Drew became the starter and had to lock in, it ended up just being Phillip and I on game days," Flutie remembers.

The pre-Rivers competitions evolved from throwing to kicking, with Flutie and Drew trying to best one another in a coffin-corner kick showdown. At one point, Drew upped the ante. "We did a kicking game, and Drew took it to a new level where he mimicked (Chargers punter) Darren Bennett's style," Flutie said. "It was more kicking, and that was low-score wins. You get it down to the 3, 2, and 1-yard lines with a series of four kicks each. We did that, but Bennett was an Aussie rules guy, so Drew took what Bennett was doing with the Aussie rules kick and started kicking the point of the ball and checking it up like the backspin."

While Drew would get creative in the kicking department, he learned from the master about the art of drop-kicking. Flutie took pride in his drop-kicking skills, which he displayed on the final play of his NFL career with the Patriots at the end of the 2006 season, famously converting a drop-kick that easily split the uprights off one bounce. Remarkably, it was the first drop-kick converted in the NFL since 1941. The kick made such an impact that it left the usually unflappable Bill Belichick smiling, laughing, and ultimately hugging Flutie on the sidelines. "He's got a skill, and we got a chance to let him use it," Belichick said at the time. "First time since "41, it might be 60 years again, too."

Years earlier, Flutie passed down to Drew his drop-kicking secrets. "We would get on a line because I was drop-kicking all the time messing around," Flutie said. The elder Chargers signal-caller made a practice of wrapping up his pregame warmups by delivering a drop-kick, which soon caught the eye of his protégé. "Drew was curious about the drop-kick, so he and I used to stand on a line and play catch drop-kicking to each other, 15 yards apart trying to kick it straight down the line under the control drop-kicking to each other. He could actually do it pretty good."

Six years after Flutie's immortal curtain call drop-kick, things came full circle at the 2012 Pro Bowl. You couldn't have written a better script.

Flutie was calling the game for NBC and Drew was on the field poised to impress his mentor. Flutie knew that for years, Drew wanted to attempt a drop-kick, so he suggested the Pro Bowl would present the best opportunity. This one wouldn't have a Cinderella ending though as Drew's drop kick came up short and a bit too low. "He had a bad drop. I'm sure it drove him crazy," Flutie said.

Losing at anything would always drive these two crazy and at times the competition hurt them in other ways. Shortly after Drew's rookie season, Flutie added basketball to the mix, convincing the then-rookie quarterback to tag along with him for a pick-up basketball game at a San Diego YMCA. "A buddy of mine called me and said, 'We're playing pick-up ball over at the Y, you wanna come down?' I said, 'Yeah, sure,' and I took Drew with me," Flutie said. Once there, things quickly escalated. "So we're playing pick-up basketball, I reach for a ball and a guy dives for it. I try to pull away, and his tooth catches me in the elbow. I elbow him in the mouth, and his tooth sliced my elbow open. I ended up needing like six stitches, and Drew sprains his ankle." It wasn't exactly the kind of competition the Chargers wanted to see their quarterback depth chart dive into right after the season. "Afterwards we come strolling into the training room and I need stitches, and Drew needs his ankle attended to," said Flutie. "The trainers couldn't believe it. They were looking at the two of us like we were crazy."

Flutie had seemingly met his competitive match in Drew, but he says there was one aspect of their games he couldn't compete with. "I will say this about Brees' skill set," Flutie marveled. "He threw the tightest spiral of any quarterback I've been around. That's the one thing he did better than anybody. If he just stood there and threw from here to there, it's gonna be a tight-ass spiral." The ole man got a kick out of how much the young gun took pride in one of his top talents. "He really threw a tight spiral, and he knew it," Flutie said, acknowledging that Drew would get the best of him in these battles. "He was lights out because when I would throw the ball, I'm really wristy in my action, so for me to throw a tight spiral, I gotta throw the ball hard. Drew was mechanically sound."

The younger quarterback liked to tease old man Flutie, who was set in his ways. So much so that the veteran quarterback earned the nickname "Salty Dog," because he was so prone to being quick-tempered when anything would change day to day, either in the game plan or from the Chargers coaching staff. Flutie said the name didn't bother him but he admitted that he did indeed get salty from time to time. "I was set in my ways, I was the old guy," he said. Flutie remembers many instances of him getting salty around Drew, but one that immediately came to mind was when Chargers Offensive Coordinator Brian Schottenheimer tried to change up the quarterbacks' warmup routine. "We're in the middle of the offseason, and Brian's new," Flutie remembers. "He's a 29-year-old quarterback coach trying to make a name for himself, and I'm 41 at the time. We're out there, one of our first offseason workouts, and he's got a jump rope, and we're all jumping rope and timing it. Finally, I took the rope, and I flipped it to Brian and said gimmie a damn football. I said, you know what jumping rope gets you good at? Jumping rope! Gimmie a football."

Drew had a front-row seat to Flutie's salty ways. "I would walk back with Drew, and I'd be like, 'You know, let's just leave the damn six route as the six route. Why are we changing because it was (previous Chargers head coach) Norv Turner's system?' We were changing things like a four route to a six route and a six to a four for some reason. Anything like that would aggravate me, any change. I was 42 years old, I don't want change, I want what I want."

The "salty" moniker became another competition chip in the quarterback room. During the offseason when Drew was vacationing in Hilton Head, South Carolina, he visited a Salty Dog Café and proceeded to have them send a "Salty Dog" football to him so he could tease Flutie. The salty football was an homage to the salty veteran, and it was at the core of a new rule for the quarterbacks that they created the following season. "Whoever was the salty dog of the day had to sign the ball," Flutie said. "I fought it, tried to censor myself at first and then we'd (the quarterbacks) all have a signature and finally I didn't care. If I'm gonna be salty, I'm gonna be salty, so my name was all over the ball."

Drew was never called salty by his teammates in New Orleans, but everyone who played with the Saints quarterback knew of his competitive nature. I remember doing a story in Training Camp every year the Summer Olympics were taking place, where I would conduct an "unscientific" poll around the locker room to see who the team thought would make the best Olympian? In the summer of 2008, during the Beijing Games, I took my first poll, and linebacker Scott Fujita was the overwhelming winner. Fujita had a reputation for being talented in a variety of sports. Before I revealed the winner on-air, I took Drew aside before we went on camera and told him what I was doing. I asked him whom he thought received the most votes? He asked, "Is it me?" I said no and told him it was Fujita. His facial expression instantly changed showcasing his usual competitive fires as he seemed legitimately upset, not that Fujita won but that he hadn't.

Four years later, in 2012, the vote for best Saints Olympian was a lot closer. Again, the votes went back and forth. It was Drew, Saints tight end Jimmy Graham, more Drew, more Graham until ultimately Graham won the vote and accepted the five-dollar medal I had purchased for the winner. I asked Drew about Graham edging him out at a press conference, and the Saints quarterback immediately fired off this retort where the ultimate competitor raised the stakes. "If you want to put together a ten-event Olympiad between me and Jimmy, I'm game," he said. Then, after a brief pause, he added, "Let's do it."

The way he said it, you felt Drew was confident he would be victorious.

Graham looked up to Drew the way Drew looked up to Flutie, but just like the two quarterbacks, the young tight end savored winning any competition against Drew, even a hypothetical one. After a Saints training camp practice, we had a simulated Olympic gold medal ceremony where I put the medal around Graham's neck, telling him of the honor and that he had bested his quarterback. "I always wanted to win a gold medal, but you never wanna tug on Superman's cape," Graham said. But what was his reaction to Drew's challenge at the press conference? "I'll definitely challenge him," Graham said. "I'll let him win a couple to help out his confidence a little bit."

While Graham was having fun with his quarterback, Drew's teammates never let him win any competition. It was evident in the Saints' daily ping pong showdowns inside the locker room. The table tennis battles were fierce and broken down extensively. They included a grading system among the players who closely monitored the rankings, which were constantly in flux. Admittedly, Zach Strief was not the best ping pong player on the Saints. But he could hold his own and was shocked Drew would be a part of the fun because of the daily demands of the quarterback's schedule.

"The locker room is not a place that we spent a lot of time with him. Practice ends, we go in, grab a recovery shake, go into the locker room, start taking equipment off and play ping pong, shower up. It's kind of a hangout. But Drew is on the field for another 45 minutes and then he's working out. He comes in, and he's got to do the media. He wants to get a 30-minute nap in every day. He didn't have a lot of time in there. I would say that Drew was not a big part of the locker room, the actual physical locker room, because he was always doing something different than us. That's just the truth, so him even playing ping pong was unusual."

It all changed one day when Drew surprised Strief and his teammates by stepping into the fray. "So Brees comes in one day, and I had just won," Strief remembers. "(Drew says) 'Alright Striefer, let's play.'" Strief and his teammates knew Drew's first sport growing up in Austin, Texas, was tennis, where he was a standout player and at one point had beaten a rising star in the area named Andy Roddick, who went on to become an elite professional. "So Brees comes over, and you're talking about a guy who was a tennis player, so there's some correlation there. And it was fairly evident in the way that he played. For a guy that doesn't play (ping pong), you could see Drew was probably a big forehand guy. That's what he was hitting. It's all he was hitting, it's all he had, but he was good. The problem was that was just an easy spin for me, so I didn't have a hard time with it."

Strief sensed a matchup problem with him and his quarterback from the start as the offensive lineman was effective offensively and defensively. Strief could return all of Brees' forehands and offered a unique spin on his serve. "We played one game, and I beat him pretty bad," Strief said. "We played a second game, and I won that one, too."

Drew concurred. "Yeah, he beat me the first couple of times we played. I could not return his serve. He had some kind of funky spin on it," Drew said.

After the win, the Saints offensive lineman wasn't protecting his quarterback. He was reveling in his victory against a teammate who rarely loses. "So that ends, and I'm kind of ribbing him a little bit, right, 'That's a really good try, I'm no Andy Roddick,'" said Strief, who smiled while reciting the Roddick comment, one he wished he had said during the game as Brees wasn't happy afterward. "He kind of tossed the paddle on the table in disgust," Strief remembers. "He didn't slam it, just kind of tossed it, then turned and walked away. There was no like, 'Good game' or anything. He just kind of left. And so the ribbing kind of goes a little more, and then I went home and didn't think twice about it."

The same cannot be said of Drew. Two weeks later, he returned to the locker room with revenge on his mind. "I came into the locker room right after practice, and Drew was in the locker room already, which is very unusual, and he's like, 'Striefer, let's go?' There was no, 'Hey, you want to play? He's ready for his rematch, and now he's a completely different type of ping pong player, completely different. All of a sudden, there's a backhand, and there's different serves."

What changed in those two weeks? I asked Drew about it once rumors began to surface suggesting that he was so upset about losing to Strief that he researched his serve by watching how other experts did it.

"So there was a guy or two who served like him, so I had to play those guys a couple of times," Drew said.

I asked him how he found those guys, but he didn't want to reveal his sources.

"You just watch, and so when I came back to play (Strief) again, I had him a little overconfident, I had him thinking I've got the spin and I can always put on it if I need to win a point and all of sudden I start returning him (says smiling) and flipped the table on him a little bit."

It was classic Brees. Just like he didn't share intimate details of his off-season routine, he wasn't about to reveal his two-week plan to unseat Strief in ping pong. To this day, it remains a mystery how the Saints quarterback turned his table tennis game around, even to Strief.

"So I don't know that Drew ever really has admitted that there was a process involved in him figuring out ping pong enough to get a rematch, but I can assure you something was done because he was a completely different style of player," Strief said.

The former Saints lineman is certain his quarterback received some quality intel behind the scenes to mount his comeback.

"I buy all of that, that all makes perfect sense, because that's very much how he is," Strief said. "He probably asked some questions (around the locker room to get a scouting report). It doesn't surprise me that he asked around, that he watched, and it was all simply to beat me, no question, you could see that."

For Drew, revenge was sweet. "I don't know where the overall stands with Strief, but I think I might be up," he said.

Strief concedes and remembers how much Brees enjoyed the rematch. "He had that smirk like, 'Oh yeah, there it is; you thought I was gonna be the same. I'm not.' I literally remember laughing and asking him, 'Have you been practicing (incognito)?' because we would know. I would have seen him playing most likely, right?"

For Drew, winning was enough. It was all he needed. No trash talk is ever involved with Brees. "No, it's personal satisfaction, it's a mental game, it's an internal game, no he's not a trash talker at all," Strief said.

Another instance in which Drew's teammates witnessed his competitive nature came at practice during a meaningless "trash can football" game between two teams led by Drew and backup quarterback Chase Daniel. The game is measured by how fast each team can matriculate the ball up and down the field by completing passes into various trash cans.

Former Saints linebacker Scott Shanle was watching this game unfold one day when the game ended up in a tie.

"For the tiebreaker, Chase was a team captain and Drew was a team captain, so we just (decided) the quarterbacks had to throw the ball into the trash can and that they would take five yards back if they kept making it," Shanle said. "Chase ended up beating (Drew) by making it from a farther distance than Drew, and we gave Drew so much crap. We said, 'Oh it's the Madden curse (Brees was on the cover of the Madden video game that year)."

The losing and the teasing didn't sit well with Brees, however.

"The next day, we come back in from workouts, and we're in the weight room, and there's a big window to the practice field," Shanle said. "Looking out the window, we could see Brees was out there throwing balls into a trash can. It was something that we all thought was over 24 hours ago, yet he's out there ticked off that he lost the game of trash can football in overtime."

His Saints teammates didn't see it as petty. On the contrary, they appreciated Drew's competitive nature and knew that it helped to make him the player he was. Having the same drive to be the best Olympian, the best at ping pong or trash can football made Drew want to be the best on Sundays and Mondays. Drew was competitive Monday through Sunday and also on Fridays, as former Saints safety Roman Harper can attest. It's not often an NFL starting quarterback has a close relationship with his safety, but his weekly competition with Harper showed Brees spread his reach all over the Saints locker room.

In one of our best postgame shows, following a 45-28 Saints playoff win over the Lions in January of 2012, I was interviewing Harper when Drew, as he would often do, stepped in and joined me after arriving early for his own interview.

Harper looked at his quarterback and on live television said, "Me and Drew we got something."

I had no idea what that something was, so I asked Drew.

"Roman and I lift weights at the same time on Friday after practice, and there is this game we play in the weight room that we kind of bet on, and then we pick a college game to go double or nothing," Drew explained. "When LSU played Alabama earlier in the year, that's when we kind of started the whole back and forth, and so It's kind of accumulated back and forth. He's up on me now, but hopefully, I'll be winning it back if LSU can get the job done."

Brees would smile and nod into the camera, where you could see the competitive fire and his hunger to get revenge on Harper. I closed the interview by saying, "That's breaking news, folks, let's see what happens? They agree tonight, but they won't be agreeing this week."

Harper then quickly interjected his customary last word by plugging his alma mater. "Appreciate it, Roll Tide."

Drew and Harper had no idea that two days later, LSU would not only lose but wouldn't score a point in the Superdome against Alabama. Harper would be the victor, another rare defeat for Brees.

Years later, Harper told me the competition between he and his quarterback started small but took on a life of its own inside that weight room on Fridays after they formed a bond over music and college football.

"That was our connection," Harper said. "I started doing three "15" Fridays. So I would go in the weight room, and every week, I would try to bench press 315 pounds. Drew would always do his extra work on Fridays, so Drew and I would be the last (players) in there, and we would have our friendly bets."

The competition ran the gamut beginning with college football and the two players' alma maters.

"We would pick five college football games every week; Purdue and Alabama had to be on the ballot and we all got points," Harper said. "We (added) another competition with these throws where we would throw a ball or roll the ball to a certain spot in the weight room."

Harper acknowledged that this was a dynamic that started small and then grew.

"It evolved over time, and it never slowed down," Harper said. "Purdue never covered, and they always get crushed. Alabama always covered, so I'm up 2-0 every week for entertainment purpose only. It was great, it brought Drew and I together, and we spent so many hours on Fridays on little stuff like that. It was great, and we did it for years."

After retirement, Drew loved looking back at the weekly in-season Friday friendly fire battles he waged with his safety but conceded that while the competition was the same, their workouts varied.

"I can promise you we were doing a different type of workout," Drew told me laughing.. "I'm over there doing core strength, joint integrity and rotator cuff exercises, and Ro is just standing in front of the mirror doing his intense dumbbell routine," Drew said smiling while mimicking what Harper was doing with his weights.

Roman told me he liked the extra Friday workout to "keep the stinger hot" a reference to keeping his arms bulked up so they would look good on Saints gamedays when he hoped everyone would take notice.

The discrepancy in workouts seemed to aid Drew in his fun competition with his safety.

"He would come out just all bulked up, which probably worked to my advantage because everything we were doing was usually like a touch game," Drew said. "Obviously, that favored me, right? I feel like I won most of those."

Where the Saints quarterback lost was in the competition surrounding the outcomes of their respective alma maters.

"Alabama and Purdue were always there with the spreads, and he always took Alabama and they may have lost one time," Drew remembered." Purdue never covered the spread, so I was always down two to zip, and there was probably seven total points to be had, right? I then had to basically go four out of the next five games to beat him, so I was always at a disadvantage. But that's ok, it strengthened the relationship."

Harper conceded who finished as the overall winner." It was me," he said confidently. "It kind of just kept going. It was more for the spirit of the game. It was just about who won or who lost, just so we could keep the game going. That's what it was all about every Friday. I was always one of the last guys in the weight room on Friday, and Drew was too. It just kind of grew from there."

With Harper it was more routine, something his quarterback routinely looked forward to. "I knew that after a practice on Friday, when the practice week is done and you're just kind of getting that last little hay in the barn, we would have our competition time," Drew said. "That's something that I honestly looked forward to every Friday afternoon, getting to that competition time with Roman."

For Drew, whether it was Harper, Daniel, Strief, or anyone else in the Saints locker room, every competition mattered, and every competition fueled him seemingly as much as the opponents in other uniforms that he faced on Sunday's and Monday's.

"You got to break up the monotony of the habitual daily grind, especially during training camp," he told me. "You had to build in those look-forward-to moments."

3

Defying The Critics

When it comes to stereotypes, Drew Brees usually deflects by calling an audible, flipping the criticism on him from a negative into a positive. When he entered the league, many thought he was too short to play quarterback. But the more success he had, the more groundwork he laid for a future generation of similar quarterbacks such as Russell Wilson, Baker Mayfield, and Kyler Murray. Wilson looked up to Drew so much as a kid growing up that he often wore a Saints cap. The Seahawks quarterback told ESPN before his first NFL meeting with Drew in 2013, "I followed him a lot. I watched him in his college career, and I remember my Dad being like, 'Man, you've got to watch this guy. This guy is awesome.'"

What Steph Curry did for a generation of young, diminutive basketball players, Drew did for undersized quarterbacks. Mayfield is a perfect example. Like Drew, the former Heisman Trophy winner grew up in Austin, Texas. And like Drew, he was a standout high school player. Yet, just as they did with Drew, the big Texas college programs ignored Mayfield because of his height.

"That's a guy that I have an unbelievable amount of respect for and looked up to just because of where I'm from first and then the size, " Mayfield said of Drew. "I've always enjoyed watching him."

Drew appreciates his role of being a trailblazer, and when I asked him about Mayfield right before Mayfield became the number one overall pick in the 2018 draft, Drew still had not met him. Nevertheless he had followed his career and seen similarities both in their stature and in their drive to make it to the NFL and prove their critics wrong.

"In following his career, I really respect what's he's been able to accomplish," Drew told me during the 2017 season. "He definitely comes across as a guy who has an edge to him and is highly competitive. You can tell there's a chip on his shoulder. You look at his career and it'll tell you why."

That sort of chip helped Drew prove the doubters wrong. He believes it helped Mayfield too. "Without question, you have to develop ways to adapt," he said. "It's the Flutie thing, right? It's that type of guy, based upon his career, based upon the fact many didn't give him an opportunity or told him all the things he couldn't do. That has motivated him or inspired him, made him and molded him into the person that he is."

The Flutie thing became the Brees thing, then erupted into the Wilson and Mayfield thing. With spread offenses and run and pass options becoming commonplace, the modern NFL is much friendlier to shorter quarterbacks than when Drew and Flutie came into the league. The one constant: these quarterbacks have had to defy the critics their entire football lives.

When Drew came into the league, Flutie helped him adjust to throwing the ball better through crowded lanes, navigating the pocket with more ease and sliding for improved field vision. Flutie admittedly is jealous of today's NFL offenses, which mirror the systems he once dominated in the CFL, where he is considered the best quarterback in league history. Returning to the NFL after eight seasons in Canada, Flutie learned many lessons he would eventually pass on to Drew, beginning with choosing the most advantageous pass protections for quarterbacks their size.

"I used to ask a lot of times, especially in Buffalo, to change protections," Flutie remembered. "Let's turn this into a slide protection. Instead of drop back, we just slide, so it creates a little more space on the front side. They can see better. Instead of doing a scat protection (where each offensive lineman has to pick up an individual defender) we would change to a slide protection."

This adjustment to more of a zone protection scheme helped Flutie become more productive during his second act in the NFL. Flutie acknowledged Drew chose a different approach when they met in San Diego. "Drew stayed deep in the pocket and stayed there and didn't use the protection thing that I did," Flutie said. "He just ran what he ran, whatever was called and (explaining it as if he was looking over tall offensive lineman) he was in the pocket and finding them."

In those early days, Flutie noticed Drew's main problem was something that would surprise many of those who followed his career in New Orleans. He had trouble staying focused. "Drew wasn't real engaged in meetings and watching the practice film and all that his first year," Flutie said. "He could nod off. Drew could actually fall asleep in a meeting as a rookie, and Brittany is probably the only one who would back me up on that because, yeah he could fall asleep anywhere."

But there was a reason for it. Drew wasn't lazy or disrespectful. He simply needed to make adjustments. He started testing his blood and finding out what he was allergic to and became very health conscious. After a myriad of tests, Drew discovered he was allergic to wheat, gluten, dairy, eggs and nuts which led him to completely overhaul his diet. The changes had Drew adding more vegetables to his meals along with a wealth of proteins. The changes dramatically elevated his energy levels where he told the Wall Street Journal in 2010, he saw a change whenever he deviated from his dietary routine. "Now when I cheat and eat things I'm not supposed to, I'll toss and turn and kick in bed and my wife knows I've been eating something I shouldn't. She has extra incentive to keep my diet in check."

Flutie saw the dietary changes Drew was making and the subsequent results. The changes were so pronounced, Drew started to eclipse Flutie in terms of eating habits.

"I'd still be stopping by McDonald's on the way to practice and stuff like that, but he figured it out (that didn't work for him, and as a result), his mental toughness became better and better," Flutie said. "He was just sharper all the time, and I relate it to that change."

Once Drew got his body and diet right, Flutie saw a different quarterback on the field and behind the scenes. "All of a sudden, he was locked in all the time and really mentally sharp and obviously physically fit."

At that moment in his career, Drew started implementing changes to his routine that one day would become the stuff of legend in New Orleans. From the way he would stay late after practice to work with his receivers to the way he would often be alone on the practice field visualizing game situations to get him ready for every moment, it was his tireless work ethic that stood out to most. "It started back prior to the 2004 season when I was with the Chargers," Drew told me. "So my rookie year was 2001. I backed up Flutie and in 2002 we competed for the job. I won the job, and we had a pretty good season in '02 and then in '03, expectations were high in San Diego, but we flopped. I got benched three times. I had a really poor season as we did a team."

After the 2003 campaign, Drew got the wake-up call that ignited the rest of his career and forced him to alter the way he approached the game.

"Going into that '04 offseason, Marty Schottenheimer, who was our head coach, basically sat me down and said, 'Listen, regardless of how I feel about you, I love you and think you're gonna be a great player. But the front office doesn't believe in you right now. They're ready to move on from you, so they're gonna go out and draft somebody.'"

The team would later use its first-round pick to select Phillip Rivers out of North Carolina State. At the time Drew wanted confidence from Schot-tenheimer that he still had a chance to win the starting quarterback job. "He said I'm the one who makes the decision, but just know you're gonna have to earn this. I said, 'Alright, great.'"

That candid conversation motivated Drew to work harder than ever. "At that moment, I made a conscious decision to do whatever I could to put myself in the best position to succeed," he said. "I'm going to take a look at every aspect of my game, from my diet to my sleep habits to all the things I probably hadn't thought of up until that point."

In typical Brees fashion, he didn't stop there. His new mindset took him places he had never experienced as a football player. It was a self-eval-uation where he opened himself up to a collection of new mentors who improved several different areas, including his preparation and the unique art of visualization, which he kept with him the rest of his career.

"We would do crazy stuff," Drew said. "We would go into a gym, and I'd blindfold myself, stand with one leg on an unstable surface and juggle and call plays. I'd literally call an entire game worth of plays and visualize and call-out coverage and tell them where I was throwing and all this stuff. And that evolved to a point where I asked myself, 'How am I gonna take this into the season and what's gonna be my routine?'"

This new and unorthodox methodology was a process for Drew, but he slowly incorporated it into his routine, which changed his approach and eventually his results.

"That routine basically came on Saturdays, when everybody is out of the building," he said. "I would walk through all the no-huddle packages in the game. I would walk through a final two-minute drive where basically we would be going down and winning the game and so I would always finish my preparation with us going and winning the game in my mind."

This approach was effective and consistent for Drew, so much so that in 2019 as his Super Bowl-winning teammates were back in town for the team's 10-year anniversary celebration, they saw a decade later what they had seen for years. Touring the facility after a Saints practice that week, former New Orleans running back Reggie Bush posted a video on Instagram he took of Drew alone on the practice field going through the motions by himself while visualizing every play in the preparation of the team's upcoming Monday night game versus the Colts. "Ain't no shortcuts to greatness," Bush posted. "This is what it's about right here. We're about 40 minutes after practice, and there's only one man out here on the field."

It was a mindset that fueled Drew and provided the winning edge he craved.

"By the time I stepped out there on the field on Sundays, it was as if the game had already been played, and we'd already won," he remembers. "I'd done everything I could to put myself and my team in the best position to succeed. It allowed me to go out and relax and play with confidence."

Trying to find that edge motivated Drew and inspired his teammates, who saw him put in the extra work from the moment he put on a Saints helmet. Teammate and Saints running back Deuce McAllister saw it even before his future quarterback entered New Orleans as they both rehabbed their respective knee and shoulder injuries together in Birmingham under the direction of the renowned orthopedic surgeon, Dr. James Andrews.

"To see how he prepared, just the rehab process, he just prepared," McAllister marveled. "We're not even teammates, so just from that standpoint, for myself, I thought he was special."

Once they were teammates, McAllister saw more of the same from a quarterback who always possessed the motivation to be the best. He immediately witnessed his new signal-caller pushing it to the limit.

"I was still rehabbing my knee, and Drew would come in early in the morning for maintenance," McAllister said. "I used to get there about 6:30,

6:45 am and, I took pride being the first one in the building. Well, one day I get there, and somebody has already beat me there, and it's Drew. So I come in the Training room, and I'm looking around like, 'Dude what are you doing? Nothing is wrong with you? And so the next day I come in, I'm about 15 minutes early, so I beat him."

The same drive to prove people wrong and be the best motivated Drew to turn the tables on Deuce.

"The next morning, he beats me again, and I basically asked him, 'What are you doin? Why are you coming to rehab,'" McAllister remembers. "(Brees) said, 'I come to get maintenance.' I was like, 'Our first meeting isn't until 8:30. Why are you so early?' He said, 'I want to be the first one in the building.'" Deuce conceded, "Ah, you won."

McAllister wasn't alone. All throughout the locker room, his Saints teammates took notice that Drew's drive to succeed was without peer.

"All I know is that, from afar, he certainly affected me," Shanle said. "He affected a lot of players and made them the best version of themselves they could be. When you see Drew in the building first, leaving last, putting in the effort that he does in the weight room, it made all of us better players. So, I always appreciated that because we were able to feed off of that. When your best player is also your most dedicated player, things turn out pretty good."

"The thing that disarms you is his work ethic," Colston told me in 2019. "When you see that guy work, day in and day out and he's there (in the building) all hours of the morning and night, that's what kind of disarms you, and it also motivates you to keep pace with him. You'll never do it, but it motivates you to try."

Drew relished being the leader and setting the tone.

"It's a joy," he said. "I love coming to work every day. I love walking in the building, seeing my teammates and just that motivation to want to go to work for them, not just with them but for them."

During the 2018 season, Saints linebacker Scott Fujita told me that he thought Drew, then 39, was playing the best football of his career. The seemingly ageless quarterback credited the time he had put in as a Saint and the process he had developed dating back to his San Diego days.

"I have lofty goals and aspirations for every season I step into," Drew told me that season. "I really just try to stay within myself. I have a great routine. I have a great thought process for how I approach each day, for how I approach the preparation, and how I approach gameday."

Despite it all, Drew's critics never seemed to go away. They lingered as he left San Diego and followed him as he started his new chapter in New Orleans. Ironically the month Drew signed with the Saints coincided with the launching of Twitter. At first, the medium was a vehicle for the fans to interact and vice versa, but eventually, it proved to be an added outlet for fans to criticize players. Over the years, Drew's critics grew and altered their focus, picking at everything from his height to his arm strength. I asked him in 2014 when he was approaching his late 30's how he and peers like Tom Brady dealt with such criticism.

Drew laughed, saying, "We both look at it and chuckle. Does it bother you to an extent? Yeah it does because people outside the building typically have no clue as to what is happening in the locker room or on the field or anything else."

The Saints quarterback had been hearing the naysayers for years. You're too short. You don't have the big arm. You can't play forever. Sure, it motivated him but at this point in his career, it just seemed to fade into background noise.

"It's obviously upon observation or things that maybe they see, but at the end of the day (smiling and slightly laughing) there's always gonna be speculation, there's always gonna be doubters, there's always gonna be crit-

ics and yet you gotta be very confident in yourself and what you're doin"
he said.

I asked Drew later in his Saints career if there was a specific criticism
of his game that bothered him the most, one that, perhaps internally, made
him want to prove the critics wrong? Drew smiled and then started laughing as if he's been down this road many times and has grown a thick skin.

"I don't know," he said. "I chuckle whenever the pundits want to say, it
could be anything."

I follow up, but what is the one thing? The smile left Drew and his tone
turned serious as he passed on a mindset that served him well in Austin, at
Purdue and in both San Diego and New Orleans.

"No, there's an attitude and a confidence and a respect that I go to the
field with and an edge every time I step on the field," he said. "It really
doesn't have anything to do with those that may have said something that
week about my game or anything else, you know."

For context on his critics, in one of our interviews, Drew inserted my
name as an example in terms of how often he allows his critics to enter his
mind when he takes the field.

"It's not like when I'm buckling up my chinstrap, I'm like, I'm gonna
prove Mike wrong this week," Drew said smiling.

Playing with a chip has served Drew well, but he understands what
issues could develop if you play the game with those critics in your head.
"Yeah, cause then I think you just play angry," he said. "I want to play like I
always have something to prove. I'm not trying to prove it to whoever said
that. I'm proving it to myself. I'm proving it to my teammates. Those are
the guys I care about."

With the same vigor that tried blocking out the noise, Drew put forth
similar energy to play for his fans where it was always apparent the impor-

tance he put into winning for his fanbase. A big part of his legacy will be lifting the yearly expectations of Who Dat Nation, and Drew was proud of this distinction, so much so, he wanted the black and gold faithful to demand the same standard he and Sean Payton set. He took it as a challenge once he raised the bar to meet those demands each week.

"Listen, there are high expectations," he said. "I feel our fan base wants us to win as much as we do. Is there disappointment? Is there that kind of feeling of, 'What the heck is going on when you kind of enter some of these tough times?' Yeah, that's a natural human emotion."

Drew understood the loyalty from his rabid black and gold fan base but also wanted to provide some perspective.

"I've always said this about our community and our fan base: If you're overreacting to this after everything we've been through together, let's just take a step back, take a deep breath and say, 'We're gonna be alright. If there's anybody that can overcome that challenge, it's us.'"

Sure, Drew fed off his critics, but those close to him appreciate how he used it to fuel himself, especially at the end of his career.

"He will never say that it drove him to have people say that he was not tall enough, didn't have a strong-enough arm, (but) that stuff remained with him forever," Strief said. "There's an edge to him. If you don't think for the last three years (of his career), him getting older and finding new ways to be productive was not a result of him with an internal desire to prove people wrong, there's no question."

4

The Payton Factor/
Game Planning

While Drew has had plenty of competitive teammates over the years, he met his match from a coaching standpoint in Sean Payton. The two will forever be intertwined as one of the top coach-quarterback tandems in NFL history. Their kinship to compete provided a special connection from the start.

"They challenge each other," said Marques Colston, who caught more touchdowns than any other player in the Payton/Brees era. "Sean is ultra-competitive just like Drew, and I think they continued to motivate each other where (they) gotta prove it to themselves and prove it to one another. When you have two guys that have that kind of football IQ, that's when you see that kind of innovative offense."

It was an offense that was seemingly great from the start, but not quite. The magic that Drew and Payton developed took the team to an improbable NFC Championship game in their first season together, but its true beginnings were rough and nerve-wracking. Drew was coming off a potentially career-ending shoulder injury, and it took him a few weeks to find his groove in his first training camp with the Saints.

"I don't think Drew could throw a ball 20 yards at that point," Roman Harper said in reflecting on his first impression of his new quarterback as a rookie in 2006.

His quarterback had the same doubts early on.

"I remember going into that training camp, and obviously, my shoulder was very much day-to-day, "Drew told me. "I can remember a couple of routes on-air sessions where I'm like bouncing the ball to Saints wide receiver Joe Horn. I'm just sitting there going, 'Gosh, come on shoulder, trust the process.'"

It was a nervous time for Drew and his new head coach as Payton was getting his first glimpse of his new quarterback. The uncertainty was palpable daily at the beginning of their first Saints camp together in steamy Jackson, Mississippi. Drew sensed the uneasiness from his head coach as he was trying to get his shoulder back in the groove.

"Talking to Sean Payton, he looked to Pete Carmichael (the Saints' new Offensive Coordinator), who was with us in San Diego," Drew remembers. "(Payton) would say, 'Is this it? Like, are we there yet? And Pete's like, 'There's more, there's more in the tank, don't worry.'"

After a rough start and fighting through the most significant injury of his career, a turning point came at the perfect time for Drew and the offense in the Saints' crucial third preseason game. The so-called dress rehearsal has the starters seeing the most action, and these Saints were trying to rebound from an embarrassing 30-7 loss to the Cowboys in Shreveport, where Drew was an un-Brees-like 7 of 12 for only 67 yards passing.

With the Superdome still not ready with its post-Katrina renovations, the game took place in Jackson at Veterans Memorial Stadium. A lot of the hype surrounded the return of Peyton Manning to the state where his father Archie is a football icon. I remember being the sideline reporter for this game where Archie was the color analyst. I was with both father and son pregame, and you could feel how special the moment was for the Manning family.

"I was excited when the game came out on the schedule," Peyton Manning said. "I knew my Dad had some of his biggest wins in college in this stadium. We've got fans who really have an appreciation for football in this town, and I was proud to be able to say I played well in this stadium."

Peyton Manning played well, leading three early scoring drives, but the other Payton would receive the best news on the night. Finally, his quarterback had officially regained his mojo. Despite Drew overthrowing two deep balls for picks and Payton saying postgame, "We're not a ready product right now as you guys can see," and newly-acquired linebacker Scott Shanle calling his wife afterward and proclaiming, "I don't think we're gonna win a game," Drew had finally found what he was looking for the previous few weeks.

Unbeknownst to many, including his teammates, the magic moment arrived in the first half against the Colts. "There was a moment in that game where I was throwing this deep out. We call it deep Q, an 18-yard route to Donté Stallworth, and I remember when the ball came out of my hand, it was like (he snaps his finger for emphasis) that was it," Drew recalled. "It was like "it." I had not felt it up until that moment."

Maybe the only one besides Drew who knew that Drew had turned the corner was his head coach. The brand-new quarterback made sure to communicate the breaking news after the game.

"I remember going into Sean's office, very upbeat, very positive, and yet it was as dejected as I've ever seen Sean because here we are probably five weeks into camp, and he's probably thinking what we're thinking, which is we may not win a game," Drew said.

Drew remembers Payton being so upset during the game he made the starters work a little overtime. "We were only supposed to play two series in that game, and Sean (left us in there), basically telling us, 'I'm leaving you in there until I tell you that's enough.'"

After the game, Drew provided Payton with a silver Saints lining, though, news he had gotten his confidence back.

"I just said, 'Coach, I know that was not a good performance all the way around, and I know we got whooped, but I'm just telling you I felt it, I just want you to know, I felt it,'" Drew said.

At the time, Drew wasn't sure his new leader was buying it as he recaptured the moment with me while mimicking how Payton received this news, squinting his eyes in disbelief.

"He kind of looked at me, like, 'Ok,'" Drew said. "Now he tells me that it meant a lot to him, where it was obviously a good sign. For me, that was it, I knew at that point I was gonna come back, and I was gonna be as good as I ever was or as healthy as I ever was, so that was a big turning point for me."

Drew knew the future was bright but could never have imagined how gleaming the following years would be with him and Sean Payton. I found interviewing him over the years that his confidence never waned, unlike some quarterbacks who have been with the same head coach for years. Interviewing him in 2014, in the middle of three straight 7-9 seasons and right after a loss that put the Saints at 4-6, Drew summarized his relationship with his head coach.

"We're two of the most confident and positive people you would ever be around," Drew told me. "It doesn't mean the losses don't hurt, or the things that surround us don't bother us. But I think it's our mentality of always glass half full, always of, 'Hey what do we have? We can, we do.'"

Drew always believed in the Payton approach and its impact on him and his teammates. He understood the modus operandi, which was and still is: "Let's put our guys in the best position to succeed, according to their strengths, and instill a lot of confidence in them."

This belief in his head coach and the system was always evident and it resulted in unprecedented success. In their 14 years together, Payton and Drew produced nine winning seasons in which they rewrote the NFL record books and won the franchise's first Super Bowl. Payton set the tone for Drew by establishing big expectations through accentuating the details. "Sean, in being the head coach in the way he addresses us and certainly as the play-caller, understands how a word or phrase or a play call can impact the team in a positive way in regards to momentum or just kind of an infusion of confidence and certainly for me as well, a guy who's pulling the trigger," Drew said. "So we take that responsibility very seriously."

The two had never met before Payton courted Drew in free agency in 2006. At the time, the team was giving both men something they hadn't had before. Payton was getting a head coaching job and Drew was getting a chance to be the starting quarterback, the quarterback of the future, a position he never wholly garnered in San Diego.

Sean Payton brought with him traits that he learned from his mentor, Bill Parcells, in Dallas, where he had been the Cowboys offensive coordinator. But unlike Parcells, who was famously tough on his quarterbacks, you rarely saw Payton and Drew exchange words on the sidelines. Instead, from the start, they got each other.

"I know his mentality, I know his positivity, I know his drive to get this thing turned around," Drew said of Payton in 2014. "He's never shied away from taking responsibility, accountability, and then letting guys know what needs to be done to fix it. He does a great job of communicating that to us."

Both men hate losing and have played the same position. Payton was a standout quarterback at Eastern Illinois and later as a replacement player in the NFL. He also had a brief stint as a quarterback in the CFL and overseas. When they met, they were close in age, with Payton being in his early forties and Drew in his late twenties. Looking back, I asked Drew how they were truly alike?

"We both see the positive in tough situations," Drew said. "I'd say that's the biggest similarity. Something I always see in him is a ton of positivity and he's always trying to draw that out of really tough circumstances."

Drew didn't stop there. He noted that while both are optimistic, both like to push the pedal to the metal. The quarterback always appreciated his coach for his penchant not to hold back,

"The aggressive nature, just kind of that confident, aggressive mentality when it comes to game day and trying to seize those opportunities when we see them and just kind of having that go for it attitude, I'd say those are the biggest similarities," Drew said.

The proof is on the field, whether it was Drew convincing Payton to go for the crucial score at the first half of a pivotal road game at Miami during the Super Bowl season or Payton in Miami a few months later calling for an onside kick to begin the second half. The Saints quarterback both appreciated and loved the fact he and his head coach weren't shy about taking chances.

So they are alike in many ways, but I asked Drew, "How are you different than Sean Payton?" The quarterback immediately pointed to their approaches. "If you look at gameday demeanor, I know we kind of get revved up in our pregame chant before the game," he said. "But after that, I gotta bring my heart rate down to a level where I can be very even keel. Good, bad doesn't matter. I'm gonna be even, poised and ready for whatever can come my way, constantly thinking and accessing and being ready for the next situation."

For Drew and Payton, body language was paramount. They didn't want to give the opposition an edge by showing any signs they had gotten the best of them. With that mindset, Drew knew his head coach possessed a different demeanor as the game unfolded.

"Obviously, Sean as a head coach has a lot going on. He's the play-caller, he's also trying to help manage the defense and special teams and communication between coaches and players, who might be injured, who's down; he's got the trainer coming up to him saying so and so's down, which might change a personnel group," Drew explained. "There are so many things that are going on in the life of a head coach on game day. He's also dealing with the officials at times so he can get pretty fired up, like headsets coming off, faces turning red, and he's laying into somebody. But for me, my mentality, my demeanor on game day is a bit more calm."

The best moment I ever had on television was with Sean Payton. The Saints had just won the NFC Championship game and were headed to the first Super Bowl in franchise history. Outside the locker room, we had to wait for the league-mandated cooling-off period to pass before we interviewed the players and coaches, but just in the nick of time, Payton's good friend, legendary singer Jimmy Buffett walked up, and I asked him to join me? He didn't hesitate. That would have been enough, but halfway through the interview, Payton joined us live by kissing Buffett and bringing in the NFC Championship trophy, too. It was live TV gold.

I had never seen that side of Sean Payton. I'd seen the easy-going side of him only in spurts here and there, but I knew he liked to have fun away from coaching, so I asked Drew to take us away from the often-monotonous press conferences and tell me about the real Sean Payton? What is he like behind the curtain? What does the public rarely get to see?

"The wheels are always turning with Coach Payton," Drew revealed. "And I'm telling you like to the most minute detail. To the average person saying why does that matter, well it matters to Coach Payton because every little thing in-regards-to the team from asking guys at the team meal while we're on the road about a hotel. 'Hey, you guys like this hotel? You think we should stay here again? How did you like the beds? The entrance that we came in? Food good?' Making sure that all of that is good, 'cause if it's not, we're gonna get it fixed.'"

Drew said Payton's attention to detail wasn't restricted to the team hotel. He was equally focused on every aspect of the football team and wanted the players' input on several subjects.

"'How do we like the travel sweatsuits?'" Drew noted. "'Are they comfortable? Do you like the colors? Ok, good.'"

Drew enjoyed breaking down the thoroughness of his longtime head coach, offering up many examples of Payton making sure the team had everything it needed.

"'Hey, let's get this recovery gear that we're gonna wear on the way home. I think that will help speed up recovery,' he'd say. He'd ask us, 'How's your sleep? Are we getting enough sleep? The statistics show you don't get a good night's sleep a couple of nights in a row. You're 20% more likely to get injured in practice because your body hadn't fully recovered.'"

Like Payton, Drew is attentive to details, too. It's one of many ways in which they are alike. Sometimes you could even see it in his facial expressions and hear it in his voice. He valued how his head coach looked out for him and his teammates in a multitude of ways.

"All of these things that are constantly coming out, he's wanting to gather information from guys," Drew said. "He wants to put us in the best position to succeed. At the end of the day, he wants to do what's best for the team, so we can win more football games. That's what you want in a head coach."

I've seen the fun side of Payton, his relationship with musicians like Jimmy Buffett and Kenny Chesney. I've seen how he sends the media ice cream for Christmas every year. But how much of that side has Drew seen? I wondered and so I asked him how often Payton mixes fun with football?

"He does, completely," Drew told me. "He's kind of a work-hard, play-hard kind of guy. He loves those moments of levity, those humorous opportunities, whether it's a story to kind of drive home a point or a message or just a laugh to loosen guys up or throw up a video or picture."

When discussing the playful side of Payton, a story stood out for the Saints quarterback. In October of 2015, longtime assistant Joe Vitt confronted two car burglars in New Orleans. The burglars eventually fled, but not before Vitt had suffered a torn Achilles tendon and a broken wrist. It kept him sidelined for weeks at Saints practices, where he watched from a scooter that he rode in an effort to stay off his injured leg. At the time, Sean Payton said in a press conference, "Joe Vitt is on the injury report."

Drew passed on to me how the message was conveyed behind the scenes in team meetings.

"Obviously, we had a field day with Coach Vitt this year," Drew told me in 2015. "His run-in with some burglars. We've had three or four occasions when a Joe Vitt slide would come up, and it's some reenactment, a picture of the alleged occurrences of that evening who Joe Vitt was chasing and exactly what happened that night besides what coach Vitt would tell you. That's an example, the opportunities that coach Payton has to get a laugh and to loosen guys up. We take full advantage."

In 2014, during the Saints' first Training Camp at The Greenbrier, Payton had the equipment team replace the sponsored Chevron patch on Drew Brees' practice jersey with a Rogaine patch. It was a dig at his quarterbacks' receding hairline. Drew liked it so much he tweeted it out.

It was a relationship built on humor and communication, yet the core of it was always a common ground on an offense tailor-made for Drew's' talents. From the beginning, the quarterback had unique input from his head coach. That was a factor his mentor Doug Flutie had told him back in San Diego would always be key if he were ever to have success moving forward.

"I think the one thing I taught him and the one thing I believe is that to take ownership of your offense in the game planning aspect of it because I didn't do that early in my career," Flutie said. "I did it late, and it's important to put yourself in a good position. You want to know what plays are going to be called in what situations, and you gotta have an input on that."

When Flutie handed down those pearls of wisdom to Drew, the veteran quarterback had no idea the career-changing impact Sean Payton would one day provide. Flutie's example was helpful to Drew and would set the tone for his Saints career.

"When Drew was struggling in San Diego, I'd always go each week and put a list of my top 10 plays and give them to the coach and say if I get in the game, just stick with this stuff. I know it like the back of my hand. I won't make a mistake.," Flutie remembered.

In terms of game planning, Flutie passed on to Drew the notion of keeping football simple. "It doesn't have to be rocket science, it doesn't have to be so intricate. It's something you have to have 100 percent belief in where everybody knows their responsibilities, and everyone is gonna feel secure, that to me is the most important aspect," Flutie said. "That and taking ownership and saying what is gonna be called, I think I influenced him a little bit there, and he became a little more hands-on." Sean Payton eventually provided all of this for Drew in New Orleans.

Flutie admits he was envious of Drew's situation with the Saints on a few fronts. For starters, he was playing primarily in the shotgun formation, which helped him see the field better.

"When Drew got to New Orleans, it was 100 percent back there, and when you spread them out, there's less pressures, more space, and it becomes easier," Flutie said. "I get a little jealous of that because a lot of that is what I did in Canada."

For Flutie, the biggest reason for Drew finding success in New Orleans was continuity. Having the same head coach and the same system for years allowed for more growth and development. It also made it easier for him to evolve. Drew, like Flutie, saw quarterbacks continually lose their coaches in the NFL, where even superstars such as Peyton Manning would have to leave teams they had been with for years. Drew knew having the same system for 15 years was rare air. With that, though, came more responsibility as the Saints playbook would continue to grow.

"I feel like every year it increases a little bit," Drew told me in 2019, describing the playbook as he expanded both hands. "You take 13 years with Sean in this system (he put his hands on top of each other as if he's stacking), and it's like the foundation has been laid and because the foundation has been laid we have the ability (moves both hands as he continues to pile, denoting progression) to add more."

I asked if it was the equivalent of a Payton and Brees library? "Yeah, it's an evolution," Drew told me. "There's offensive evolution and defensive evolution. You're constantly trying to stay ahead of the curve, be one of the innovators instead of one of the copiers."

This mindset took years to develop, where the Payton and Brees' playbook was akin to a law book that they continually relied on precedence in constructing current game plans.

"Always with the ability to go back to and reference something that took place so many years ago," Drew said. "You think would be a good fundamental to bring back into the offense whatever it might be based on personnel, based upon the defense that you're going up against or something like that."

On this subject, Drew smiled and delivered an updated example, explaining that "The more weapons like Taysom Hill that you have, the more play calls you have to memorize. Now I have to remember where I'm lining up at receiver which is a little bit different."

A Collaboration

Drew appreciated the library he had built with his coach and knew a key in-game planning was gathering input from his teammates on what worked for them. The Saints quarterback didn't watch tape with his offensive lineman in New Orleans but made sure each week after their respective tape sessions that he would get together to make sure everyone was on the same page. The quarterback had the mindset just because he saw it one way didn't mean that's how his linemen were reading it? It was always a collaboration in terms of Drew telling his linemen; this is how I see it, are you guys seeing it the same way? If the answer was no, the linemen wouldn't adjust, Drew would.

"There was a constant dialogue of how we saw certain pressures," Strief said. "Drew was always very easy to get to adjust to how it worked best for us. I can remember times where we were getting a certain pressure, and Drew's like, this is what I'm gonna say. I'm gonna down this guy, and I'm gonna send you guys over here, and we're like, "Uh, that doesn't make sense, why don't you just packer it (shift to another protection). But he's come to a point after extensive film study that this is what he's gonna do, this is what he's decided. Then he shares it with us and we're like, 'Uh, we don't like it.' And there was never any hesitation. It was always like, 'Ok, I gotta fix my brain right to make it easier for them.'"

The collaboration process helped make the offense the best in NFL history, where Drew knew the constant communication helped the unit avoid any breakdowns.

"That was pretty constant, and I would say consistent," Strief said. "There was always a dialogue between us and him that we were comfortable with everything he was doing and how he saw defenses."

In addition, Drew's lineman appreciated the fact he always put them first. "I think he knew, it's easier, and I trust more that I'm gonna change it and make it so that it's easier on them than having them adjust to me. There was never adjusting to Drew, it was always Drew adjusting for us," Strief said.

Drew was always trying to get his offense on the same page from his lineman to his wide receivers. His ability to make his teammates better was evident in the growth of his targets. The Saints quarterback put up huge numbers year after year, often without many household names around him. The bulk of his tenure in New Orleans found him building chemistry with players who weren't drafted, such as Lance Moore, Pierre Thomas, and Colston, a late seventh-round pick who became his favorite target. In fact, Drew didn't have a Pro-Bowl wide receiver until Michael Thomas in 2017, his 12th season with the Saints.

While Thomas was the first, a case can be made that Colston should have been. No other receiver in Saints history put up better numbers, and he was undoubtedly Drew's favorite target, amassing nearly ten thousand receiving yards, 711 catches, and 72 touchdowns. Drew made Colston a focal point of the offense immediately in New Orleans, sparking a relationship that matured over their decade together. "There's a certain level of trust that we built over ten years together," Colston reflected. "There were times where, you know, we would just see the field the same way, making it up as we went along. To build a relationship and build a rapport with somebody like that man, those are things you can't replicate."

Colston is quiet and extraordinarily modest, but his early play made more prominent players such as Donté Stallworth and Joe Horn expendable. Drew proved he could get the best out of Colston and the core of receivers such as Moore, Robert Meachem, and Devery Henderson, who were the recipients of the best years of the Brees era. It was a rare chemistry that allowed Brees and his favorite targets to put up elite numbers, but those same receivers never replicated the same success outside of the Big Easy. Colston acknowledged that the chemistry was unique. The Saints' elite quarterback and his receiving corps were together for so long they knew where they had to be, and their quarterback would routinely find them. "Yeah, there were a bunch of those times," said Colston. "We had this saying, stemming from (former Saints quarterbacks' coach) Joe Lombardi: there are rules guys and guidelines guys. There were certain things that Lance and myself were able to do. We became guidelines guys. These are kind of the parameters that you play in. Whatever you do here, make sure it works," Colston said.

"We were all learning this offense together in 2006, then Meachem came in in 2007," Lance Moore said. "So I guess over time it just developed into, ok, the young guys that come in and don't know this offense or the guys we traded for, they're gonna have to be rules guys, right. We can't let them go off on a tangent and do their own thing because it kind of messes everything else up."

"I consider myself so blessed, so fortunate, that when I first got there in '06, and then really from '06 to '13, Marques Colston was there; Lance Moore was there, Devery Henderson was there, Robert Meachem was there," Drew told me. "To literally have the same four guys for that stretch was special, and for the most part, those guys stayed pretty healthy."

It took time for Drew to build this chemistry, though, as Colston admits, "but the rookies coming in, you were the rules guys, whatever that playbook looks like, that's what you do." Drew's favorite target saw how experience benefited him and the longtime core of receivers he played with

"Just to be in the offense for that long, to build that rapport, you're seeing the field through the same set of eyes, that's nothing but repetition and trust," he says. "It was a special, special moment in time and the fact that moment lasted (10 years), you just don't see that, man."

Growing Pains

The lowest point of the Brees and Payton era were the three straight losing seasons from 2014 to 2016. Drew admittedly did some soul searching then, wondering how many more years he had left. But the 2017 draft class and the season that followed reignited his hunger along with the proficiency of the Saints offense. At that point, he realized he no longer had to do everything for the team to succeed. The Saints in the Brees era were always better when the offense could run the football. You saw it in the Super Bowl season and the subsequent record-setting years in 2010 and 2011. It was also apparent in 2017 with the arrival of the one-two punch of Mark Ingram and Alvin Kamara. Drew told me in 2017 how much that emerging dynamic made his job more manageable.

"While my job responsibility is the same as far as getting us in the end zone and taking care of the football, the description as to how that is done has changed a little bit, and you understand the flow of the game too," he said.

For example, Drew referenced the Saints 47-10 blowout of the Bills in Buffalo in 2017. Looking at the score, you would have thought he had one of his best days. In reality, Drew had more rushing touchdowns (one) than passing touchdowns (zero, remarkably). The Saints running backs took the load off their veteran quarterback that day by rushing for 298 yards.

"We get into a game like Buffalo, where we're running it seven to eight yards a pop," Drew said. "I don't have to take chances. You know that would decrease our chances of winning the game for me to take chances."

The 2017 season revitalized the Saints quarterback where his comments to me a few years later were revealing as he compared his feeling that year to the previous three straight losing seasons.

"In years past, I'll be honest, I had to take chances," he said. "I had to take chances in order for us to move the ball to make the type of plays that we need to score enough points to win the game. You're always conscious of what you need to do to put us in the best position to win the game. Whether we're running it in or throwing it in, I don't care. I just want us to score points, and I just want us to win."

Team Chemistry

It was clear talking to Drew how much of a toll those three straight losing seasons took on both himself and the organization. The game plan wasn't in sync and neither was the locker room, which included malcontents such as Brandon Browner and Junior Galette. It was a stark contrast to what the Saints had built between 2006 and 2011, where leaders were bountiful.

"We had some tough years here," Drew told me in 2017. "You know, the last three years in trying to re-establish ourselves and rebuild the foundation and go out and get the right type of guys here. We put a huge value on character, toughness, and intelligence. I feel we've done that, and now we're reaping the benefits of that because we have the right type of guys in the building."

In 2017, Drew was excited about a fresh start with a better locker room full of reliable veteran leaders and several talented up-and-comers.

"We certainly have a window of opportunity with the guys that we have, and there's so much that goes into that," he said. "You know the ability to stay healthy, keep guys on track, keep guys improving and motivated.

I think the sky's the limit for this group. I do. I think we have guys in key positions, in key roles that are locked up for a period of time where, this is our window, this is our opportunity to really make a run at it."

Payton and Drew never possessed the rebuilding mindset, not even during their first year together in 2006 when the team was seemingly starting over after coming off a 3-13 season with a rookie coach and a quarterback returning from a potentially career-ending injury. Looking back on that, Drew told me in 2016 that there were lots of questions when this union started.

"Yeah, you go back to 2006 and we were all just trying to figure it out and maybe not knowing what we got ourselves into at the time," he said.

But the Saints quarterback who was at his career crossroads liked the message being sent from the onset by his head coach.

"Sean and Mickey (Loomis, the Saints General Manager) tried to piece together a football team that could be competitive, but we were really just beginning to lay the foundation for the type of team and type of character that they would want to build around."

Drew liked the early message and loved the chemistry of those early Saints teams in the Payton era.

"I'll be honest with you. I think everybody on the '06 team would agree, (we) probably weren't the most talented, the most sought-after guys when you looked around the league at free agency and everything else. We've been the castaways and a bunch of other things, guys who had no other place to go or very few choices, and yet we all ended up in New Orleans together for a reason, for a purpose, for a common cause."

A cause where both men clicked immediately in terms of the playbook, their unique communication as a head coach and quarterback translating into a rare chemistry that spread throughout the Saints seemingly from day one.

"It's pretty awesome to go back to '06," Drew said. "You talk about start-ing from scratch. Sean Payton comes in (where) I don't think people fully realize (outside of New Orleans) what this city had gone through with Ka-trina, really just the full-scale change of Sean Payton coming in and want-ing to literally start over and rebuild this foundation from the ground up."

The collaboration of the first Payton/Brees team was unique when you see its origins from every corner of the locker room, including both sides of the ball. For example, the Saints' three starting linebackers arrived during training camp. Veteran Scott Fujita came from the Cowboys in the offseason, but veterans Scott Shanle and Mark Simoneau joined the team at the end of the Saints' preseason.

Interestingly, they never played a game together until the Saints 2006 season opener versus Cleveland. Simoneau came aboard from the Eagles in exchange for a draft pick and veteran wide receiver Donté Stallworth, which left a further void for a young Saints offense.

"You just think about how that '06 team came together," Drew reflected to me after his career was over. "Terrence Copper, who had been a great special teams player for us and a great receiver, because Joe Horn missed half that season. Terrence Copper was our starting Z. We got Copper, picked him off waivers from Dallas, right before the season."

This patchwork Saints team had a common bond, though. They were all picking New Orleans as its second and, in some cases, third choice. Pay-ton admittedly wanted the Packers head coaching job before settling on the Saints. The Dolphins rejected Drew in free agency because he couldn't pass their physical. From new linebackers to backup wide receivers, these Saints entered New Orleans in the same boat.

"For a lot of us, it was, 'Man, it's not like we had a whole lot of options, you know," Drew said. "(Former Saints assistant head coach) Joe Vitt used to always joke around that we were the 'castaways,' this group of castaways that nobody really wanted, that man this is your opportunity, right? I think we all saw it for much more than football."

Under Payton and Brees, these Saints were more significant than football for a region that needed them in such tumultuous times. This NFL melting pot of castoffs miraculously came together to form not only a talented team but a group that had remarkable chemistry and leadership for many seasons.

"You just look at how it all came together, the right type of guys, guys that were ready to work, had a chip on their shoulder like something to prove and saw this being much more than just football," Drew said. "Obviously, that resulted in that very special '06 season, and there were some growing pains in '07 and '08, and there were some pieces to the puzzle we had to add. We go out and trade for (Jonathan) Vilma in '08 and some draft classes, but (to have) that all culminate to '09, and what you saw in '09 was that accumulation of the right type of guys, the right type of leaders and just a lot of hard work."

The Payton Process

Under Payton, Drew learned the importance of details, body language, team chemistry, and an evolving playbook. Even though he and his coach were together for 14 seasons, the process to churn out the big offensive numbers were ever-changing each season as they constantly made adjustments each week. Drew took me through the weekly cycle of laying out the game plan to set the foundation. The next step in the process would be nerve-wracking, though.

"I would say it's chaos early on because as you're watching film, there's so much to absorb," he explained. "What do they do in this formation? What do they do in this situation? What are we anticipating here? But what if they do this? So, there are all those what ifs."

Once he and Payton ironed out the many questions, it was on to plotting the execution, where the quarterback has to dissect another set of issues.

"Then it's, well here's the game plan, here's base, here's what we're doing on third down, short-yardage and goal line; here's two-minute and all these situations, right? It's chaos because there is so much information," Drew said.

But he loved the process. Drew smiled as he described it to me.

"What you have to do is throughout the week, you create order from that chaos," he said. "You try to take it section by section and just slowly compartmentalize it, which takes time."

The time he and Payton put in to fine-tune everything was a grind, one they would perfect over the years.

"So many Tuesdays, Wednesdays, Thursdays, and Fridays," Drew said while signing and waving his hands to convey the image of this myriad of information to digest. "We had all of this information, and when we got to Saturday, each one kind of has its compartment within the brain or its little slot, and then you get to game day, and it's all sitting there lined up for you, so whatever the situation is you just you just reference that file up here (points to his head) and I know what to expect. I know what my plan is. If they do this or they do that, here we go."

At this point in our conversation, I was curious about the spontaneity of the process. Were some of their best collaborations planned late in the week, even as late as Saturday night or Sunday morning? Drew laughed and said, "Yeah that has definitely happened."

I asked him to give me an example, and he quickly delivered.

"We're playing the Miami Dolphins on Monday Night Football in 2013, and we had a walkthrough at the hotel the morning of the game and we're going over the second or third play on the game script," he remembers. "We were going to the empty (back set) and it was one of those looks like, if we get that one pressure look, here's a safety or a linebacker trying to cover (Darren) Sproles on this little out route, well instead of an out route, let's give them a little out and up and try to turn it into a big play."

Fast forward to the game, and Drew and Payton got what they had anticipated.

"Sure enough we get the look on the second or third play of the game, we check to it and hit Sproles on a 40-yard pass down the sideline that sets up our first touchdown." Drew recalled.

You could see in Drew's face how much he loved the process and working with someone weekly like Payton made it even more enjoyable over the years. Their method of preparation, their shared penchant for taking chances consistently paid off. And it paid off big in that instance. When describing this example, Drew continued to smile and then held out his arms as he remembered what it was like to see all of the hard work pay off.

"I remember as it's unfolding in slow motion, just something we installed that morning, if we get this look and here's that look and here's Sproles (his smile getting even bigger), I look to the sideline and (mimics his fist pump to his head coach) to Sean, so yeah that stuff happens more than you think."

Drew Brees and Sean Payton were an unpredictable and unlikely pair, but they formed a perfect football union. Many speculate how football would have been different if Miami had signed Drew Brees back in 2006 when he was a free agent. Then Dolphins head coach Nick Saban may never have gone to Alabama? As a result, who knows how the Payton era would have been defined by a quarterback not named Drew, or if Drew would have attained the same levels of success without Payton playing for the Dolphins?

We know this, Payton and Drew together were good from the start and formed one of the best coach-quarterback tandems in NFL history, a bond the quarterback will forever be grateful for.

"I wouldn't be here if it wasn't for Sean Payton," he said. "He gets the job in January (2006). I get the call from him about a month later, and he tells me he wants me to be his quarterback and lead his team, and we're gonna do great things together, and we're gonna form this offense and do something special."

Drew was emotional when telling me about the beginnings of such a special bond, an unlikely journey between a quarterback and coach that proved to be historic.

"The evolution from that moment until now, there are just so many things that coach Payton and I can reference and reflect on from years past," Drew said. "I will always be in debt to him for having that faith and belief in me at a time where it was hard to have that in myself."

Payton and Drew built the culture of the Saints together. In my many interviews with the Saints quarterback, his words often echoed his head coach's. That was by design. These two men shared a competitive mindset, an expansive playbook, and a belief in the importance of the foundation originating with a healthy culture. Drew, like Payton, was often a better interview after a loss than a win during his career. The quarterback adopted this mindset but often, his teammates under Payton's leadership felt the same accountability in good times and bad.

"Absolutely, I've always felt, the best teams are the ones that are truly player-led," Drew told me. "You're not waiting for the coach to say something or to give you the points of correction or whatever it is. The best teams that we've had here had the type of player leadership where we knew what needed to be done, and we'd step up and get it done whether it was a practice or in a locker room or after a game."

As often as I routinely interviewed Drew, I spent several years grabbing players to go on with me after memorable nights and heartbreaking defeats. The majority of the time, the Saints' locker room led by Drew and Payton faced the music because of the standard set by both men.

"At times, you had to face some tough questions or tough criticism or whatever it might be," Drew said. "A lot of that is just the confidence in our team, knowing the type of guys that we had and, just the fact that we really did love each other, we wanted to play for each other and, we wanted to represent each other the best way that we could."

At the end of their remarkable era, Drew and Payton understood culture reigned supreme. A mindset that set the tone for all of their team success.

"It was beyond our own personal goals or representing ourself, it was really about representing our team the best way we could," Drew said.

5

Spinning Records

Looking back on Drew's career, many things stand out: his unbridled competitiveness, his incredible accuracy, his impressive longevity, and the length of pages he's added to the NFL record books. In a city known for its music, its quarterback became the ultimate DJ, spinning records seemingly at will, particularly late in his career. As the records piled up, he typically shied away from waxing poetic on his achievements, which included becoming the all-time passing leader and all-time leader in career touchdown passes, always saying that he wouldn't reflect on those marks until his career was finished.

"Each (record) stands alone and has its special place," Drew told me in 2018, shortly after topping Peyton Manning as the NFL's top passing leader. "One, I hope they're some more, and number two, I just love all the people who have been along for that ride."

It was a ride that Drew came to appreciate more as his career neared its eventual end. He savored having his growing boys ride shotgun in an unprecedented drive past some of the most impressive quarterback milestones ever. The Saints quarterback also found it special to hear from fans who were the same age as his sons. In all the interviews we did after his many record-breaking nights, the story that stands out is the interaction between a young fan in the Superdome and Drew in 2011, the night he would break Dan Marino's mark as the NFL's all-time single season passing leader. Before Drew broke that mark, the young Saints fan gave his favorite quarterback all the motivation he would need.

"Pregame, after I throw with the receivers, I stop and sign autographs for our fans in the corner (referring to the area north of the end zone adjacent to the entrance where the team runs out on the field)," Drew told me on that record breaking evening. " A little boy said, 'I came here to see you break the record tonight,' and it just reminded me of when I was a little boy watching athletes that I looked up to. I always hoped that maybe one day I would have that opportunity, be down on the field. Never in my wildest dreams did I think we'd have this opportunity, and I guess it brought me right back to that moment when I was a little kid, and it made me realize how lucky we are to be in this position (getting emotional), how lucky I am to get to play in the National Football League, quarterback of the New Orleans Saints, to live in this city and to be able to have a chance to break a record like that."

It was an emotional exchange but one that motivated Drew after he took it in.

"I got a little emotional walking back to the locker room after that," Drew told me in relaying the emotional exchange with the young fan. "I think it kinda help relax me and say, "Welp, the fans came to see it so, let's give them what they came to see.""

There were plenty of nights where Drew would deliver for the fans. Memorable nights like that became commonplace for the Saints' one-man obliterator of the NFL record books. Here are the top memories from those milestone moments:

The Unitas Record (and a San Diego reunion) October 7th, 2012

While Drew didn't want to bring attention to himself, the NFL had other plans as it adeptly scheduled Saints prime time games around his mega milestones. You could picture the league working its scheduling magic around the Saints quarterback's latest attempts at making history. The best example of this narrative was in the 2012 offseason, when Drew was knocking on the door of a record that had stood for a half-century—Johnny Unitas' record 47 straight games with a touchdown pass. The league knew Brees was only six games shy of the mark that had stood since 1960, so they used their power to produce a dandy. Brees' old team, the Chargers, were slated to play in New Orleans, so why not make this a primetime game and just maybe a record-setting night? While the league had a great knack for timing, the Saints ended up limping into this made-for-TV showcase.

Due to Bountygate, an unprecedented scandal where the Saints were accused of paying bonuses or "bounties" for injuring opposing players, Sean Payton was hit the hardest receiving a suspension for the entire 2012 season, becoming the first NFL head coach to be suspended in over 30 years for accusations of trying to cover up the misdeeds. His loss was palpable as New Orleans entered with an 0-5 record. It was a season in which NFL commissioner Roger Goodell became public enemy number one in the Big Easy. With his coach serving a one-year suspension, Drew reached out to Goodell and asked if he could make an exception and have Payton in the building when he broke Unitas' record. When I asked Drew that season about making an effort and getting permission from the commissioner, you could feel how much it meant to have Payton there for his big night.

"I mean, regardless, he would know he's always there in my heart, in my mind, even though he might not be there physically," Drew told me. "I know for him, the opportunity to be here, to see our team, albeit from a distance on the field, just to share in the moment was something that was important to all of us."

It was never lost on Drew how intertwined he and his coach were on those record-breaking nights. When he moved past Dan Marino to become the single-season passing leader, he gave credit where he felt it was due.

"He's the biggest part of this, and I certainly wouldn't have this opportunity if it wasn't for him, really believing in me when not many others wanted to," Drew said of Payton. "I think in life all we need is just somebody to believe in us, and as confident as we might be in all of those things, you just need something good to happen. Coach Payton has been that guy for me every step of the way. Every time I step on the field, I'm thinking about winning for a lot of people but none more so than Sean Payton."

Also on hand was Unitas' son, Joe, who had flown in from Las Vegas. During the week, on behalf of his family, Joe Unitas had written Drew a letter expressing the sentiments of the Unitas family, which was fully behind the man breaking their Dad's heralded mark. Indeed, in the letter, the family wrote that if anyone were to break the record, they wanted it to be someone like Drew. After the game, I had a chance to speak with Joe Unitas at length where you could sense the great appreciation, he had for a quarterback who had just broken a record his father had owned for decades.

"Of course, his ability to play the game of football is special, that's obvious," Joe Unitas told me. "But what's more important is outside of that how he utilizes maybe that pedestal he's given to do good for other people. For the community, for children, I know he's heavily involved with children's charities, and he's a father, and those are the three things that were most important to my Dad."

Drew didn't waste any time breaking Unitas' mark, establishing a new record with just over three minutes left in the first quarter. The play was full of irony as he found speedy wide receiver Devery Henderson, who ironically wore the same number 19 as Unitas, wide open on the play.

"Obviously, I didn't even think about that at the time," Brees told me when I brought up the amazing coincidence of throwing the record-breaking touchdown pass to a player wearing the same number as Unitas. "Now that you mentioned it, everything happens for a reason. No better guy to catch that ball than Devery, too, just being one of the most tenured Saints, been through so much here, really been a mainstay on this offense for so long, really one of the unsung heroes of this team."

Drew enjoyed celebrating with his teammates and while he wished Sean Payton could have been on the sidelines, he shared with me how impactful the postgame meeting was with him and general manager Mickey Loomis, who the NFL had suspended for half of the 2012 season as a result of the Bountygate scandal.

"It was great," Drew said. "Obviously they're as big a part of this as anybody, Sean Payton, Joe Vitt, Mickey Loomis. I guess I don't want to reflect too much (sounding emotional), but they're the reason I'm here. All those guys have been here for all seven years, Mickey, longer."

Drew was six years into his Saints career when he threw that record-setting TD pass, but on that night he still hadn't forgotten what the organization meant to him.

"We've been able to accomplish some great things together," he told me. "I certainly wanted them to know they were as important a part of tonight as anybody. The fact that they were all able to make it, be in this building, share in that historic moment, was special."

Ironically the Saints delivered Drew the ultimate belief in his abilities, a stark contrast to the opposite sideline that evening. The Chargers drafted his successor in Phillip Rivers and then gave up on Drew after he beat out Rivers, only to suffer a season-ending shoulder injury in 2005. Seven years later, it was Drew not only defeating his former franchise but setting one of the NFL's oldest and most treasured passing records while doing so. I asked him that night, "If you didn't go through the adversity in San Diego, do you think you'd be the quarterback you are today?"

"No, not at all," he told me after the game. "All of those things, they shape you, they mold you, they strengthen you. They allow you to become maybe what you never would become if you hadn't gone through those things."

Drew finished his Saints career undefeated versus his old franchise, beating them in London during the 2008 season, on this record night in 2012, and then again in 2016 in his lone Saints game at San Diego.

"I had five great years in San Diego," Drew told me once. "I did. I learned a lot. I had a chance to be around some great players, great coaches, and then carry that with me here and been a part of such a great journey here. Hopefully, we've got a lot more years left. I'm 33 years old, I'd love to play out this deal and another one, but we'll just take them one game at a time and keep marching on."

In our interviews, you could tell how much Drew enjoyed the moment, but he was always looking ahead and hoping his playing days would never end. He took the high road after beating the Chargers, but it was clear the wins over them meant a great deal. For example, after the 2016 victory in San Diego, his only game there as a Saint before the Chargers moved to Los Angeles, he engineered two scoring drives in the final five minutes, then told me of the victory afterward, "Yes, this one ranks way up there."

For Drew, playing the Chargers was always emotional. It was especially so in his first and only return to his old stomping grounds. The day before the game, he took time to walk out on the field at Jack Murphy Stadium by himself and reflect on his first trip back since his career-altering shoulder injury. I asked him when we were in San Diego at the time, how emotional that private moment was?

"It was (very emotional)," he said. "The last time I stepped foot in this stadium was eleven years ago, and I walked out of the stadium with my shoulder out of socket, (thinking) I may not play football again. So here we are eleven years later, and it was the first opportunity to kind of meet that fear again but with a feeling of gratitude. I just kind of walked to the spot where I got hurt, knelt down, took a moment to say a long prayer to my Lord. Just thanking him for putting me in this position, having this opportunity and bringing me to New Orleans. Really, it put a lot of things into perspective. It allowed me to reflect quite a bit. If I could sum it up in just one word, I would say grateful."

When it came to the Chargers, the competitor in Drew always wanted to beat his former team, especially in his only return to the city he still calls home in the offseason.

"This one will rank up there forever," Drew told me in our interview in San Diego. "I mean, there are a few moments that will stick out forever. This will definitely be one of them."

Sure, beating the Chargers served as a reminder of how far he had come, but in a vintage Drew moment, he didn't want to think about any possible conclusion. After the 2016 victory versus San Diego, I asked him, "You have a long plane ride home with some time to reflect. If someone had told you 11 years ago what your journey would be, what you would accomplish, it's been an unbelievable comeback story?"

Drew's response was consistent with many, whether it was a record-setting night or one of the many standout victories across his 15-year career with the Saints: "Yeah, but it's not over. (I'm) just so thankful I've had the opportunity to play this long and to make it back here to play the game."

Beating the Chargers was emotional, satisfying, and in Drew's career, historic. The 2012 win had him passing the great Johnny Unitas and setting a record which in many ways is the NFL equivalent to Joe DiMaggio's immortal 56 game hitting streak in baseball.

"Hopefully, we can keep this record for a while, as Johnny U would say," Drew told me on the record-breaking evening. "I guess records are made to be broken. I'm sure somebody is gonna break this one at some point. Hopefully, we'll be able to extend it for a while and hold on to it for awhile."

Drew would indeed extend this record to 54 straight games with a touchdown pass. You can make the case this milestone, due to its longevity, skill, and shades of luck could be the record he will hold the longest.

The All-Time Passing Leader (passing Peyton Manning) October 8th, 2018

The NFL schedule makers had complete faith in Drew Brees, so just as it did with the Chargers game in which he broke Unitas' record, the league offices scheduled a primetime matchup right around the time he was set to eclipse Peyton Manning for the title as the league's all-time leading passer. Drew entered the season that year trailing the New Orleans native by 1,495 yards, so it's obvious that the NFL executives had broken out their calculators and figured that if he averaged his usual three hundred yards plus per game, Drew would likely break Manning's record in Week 5. Unfortunately for the NFL, Manning's Indianapolis Colts weren't on the schedule that year, so it settled for a Monday Night Football meeting versus Washington.

It worked out just as well.

No quarterback in NFL history has put up better numbers on Monday Night than the Saints quarterback. According to ESPN Stats and Info,

Drew has the most career passing yards and touchdowns in Monday Night games and is tops for single-season passing yards and single-game completion percentage on Monday night. He delivered again on this historic night against Washington, opening the game with four straight scoring drives and then adding his usual flair for the dramatic. With the record in sight, Drew passed Manning by finding Saints receiver Tre'Quan Smith with a perfect pass. Smith did the rest, finding the endzone to complete a 62-yard touchdown. It was a memorable first career touchdown in Tre'Quan Smith's career. The rookie wide receiver got caught up in the moment, telling me afterward he almost threw the ball into the stands because he briefly forgot the history that was unfolding.

"My first career touchdown, and I can't get the game ball," Smith joked. "(But) I'm not mad at all. I'm going down in history, so that's a great thing. Actually, at that moment of my score, I just dropped the ball in the end zone, hopped in the stands, and I'm like, 'Why is everybody in the middle of the field?' Then I realized, and (ran) back to congratulate him and (one of my teammates asked me), 'What about the ball?' I'm scratching my head. I dropped it in the end zone and thank God, (Drew) got his ball in the end. Happy for him."

The sequence of Smith scoring and nearly leaving the milestone's football behind wasn't lost on longtime New Orleans still photographer Parker Waters, who was working from the same Superdome end zone and had a front row seat for the play and near disaster from the Saints rookie wide receiver.

"He's running at me and as he goes by in the back of the endzone where I'm kneeling and shooting, he just drops the ball and it stops right by my knees," Waters said. "I change cameras and switch to get shots from the back of the endzone of the celebration and the crowd. I look back and the ball is still there, and I go 'oh my god this is the ball, someone's going to want this ball.'"

Waters next move helped alter history and save Tre'Quan Smith. "I pick the ball up and one of the officials is running down the field trying to catch up with the play with his eyes right on me." At that point, Waters holding his newfound prized possession started to feel things moving in slow motion. "I took the ball and tried to give it to the official as if it were a baby. I was so relieved to get rid of it. Then they get the ball, they give it to Drew, he holds it for a second and they give it to David Baker (Former President and CEO of the Pro Football Hall of Fame) He's got on white gloves and accepts it and says 'this ball will never touch human hands again.'"

Waters knew differently, "I'm thinking my DNA is on the ball."

After the game, I asked Drew about breaking such a milestone with such a huge play? He admitted separating the time of the record with the play wasn't easy.

"I would say that's the worst part of this, obviously hoping this would happen and then at what point in the game is this happening," he said. "You don't want to kill momentum and all those things. First half, two-minute drive, long pass like that, (it) actually gives you a chance to soak it in with the fans, my family, my teammates, (which) was great."

Brees' family was a big part of the night as his wife Brittany and their four children made it down to the Saints' sidelines with Dad just 35 yards shy of the record.

It's a moment the Saints quarterback never envisioned in his career, but what made it the most satisfying was sharing it with his kids, whom he always hoped would be old enough to remember him playing. Drew told his children as he hugged them, "I love you guys so much. You can accomplish anything in life that you're willing to work for, right?" Upon hearing those words, many were moved, including Drew's former teammates like Scott Shanle, who later told his former quarterback, "When you went over to your kids and told them, you can have anything you're willing to work for, I've told my, kids, that."

Saints fans have seen countless videos of those Brees boys tackling each other over the years, but they were composed on this night, not only with Dad during his big moment but also after the game sitting patiently behind the cameras during our postgame show. It was way past their bedtime, but Dad had interviews to do, and they were watching intently. You could sense the excitement they all shared simply being a part of a such a momentous moment with their father. Drew's boys were all below the age of 10, yet it seemed as they watched me interview their Dad behind the camera, they knew that this night was different, that Dad had accomplished something very special.

Dad also knew the importance of incorporating his sons into such a defining moment, where it was obvious Drew wanted them to be there with him and enjoy every aspect of the evening, including our postgame show together. It was the first time the Brees boys had stayed up this late to see Dad make history. With daughter Rylen leaving after the game with Mom, it was a boys' night out for Dad's big night, and I asked Drew how much it meant to share an evening like that with his three sons? "Really special," he told me with his sons hanging on every word in the background. "I think the greatest responsibility in the world is being a father. I love the game of football. I play it because God's blessed me to play it, and I'll play it as long as I can. It's the life lessons you learn from it, things I can impart on them by bringing them around it (he leans to his sons for extra emphasis while talking), allowing them to see the way their Dad works and to see the way he interacts with his teammates and watch them work. Just to watch how all of that comes together, I certainly try to impart that on them, every chance I get."

One day, Drew's sons will see the images and the highlights and fully appreciate just how hard Dad's path was to this special night. He wasn't a big time recruit, a hyped up draft pick and was given up by San Diego, so I asked him if the rocky road made this night that much more special? He immediately deflected to those who assisted him throughout his long and winding football journey.

"There are so many people along the way that helped pave the way for me," he said. "So many people I have a ton of gratitude for, and I am just so grateful for this opportunity, and I hope all those people know how thankful I am for their influence in my life."

Those people included the Manning family. As he usually does, Archie Manning texted Drew a good luck message prior to kickoff that night. Meanwhile, Peyton Manning, as he usually does, provided some levity, sending his congratulations to Drew via a humorous skit that was shown on the Superdome jumbotron. It was meaningful as their relationship goes back to Drew's college days at Purdue.

"Yeah, we go way back," he told me that night. "He was drafted by the Colts in 1998, and I was an hour down the road at Purdue, so I had the chance to watch him play early in his career at Indy and had the opportunity to meet him, meet the family. Little did we know, we'd play against him in a Super Bowl and then obviously have these moments. It's amazing how that all comes together."

Drew could have only imagined having these kinds of nights with Manning back in their Indiana days, but all of those years later knew being viewed as a peer with one of the best of all time was meaningful.

"I feel like I'm a part of his generation of quarterbacks," Drew shared with me. "Peyton Manning was always the benchmark. He was the guy paving the way. You just felt like if he played long enough, he was going to own all of these records. But not only that, he was such a winner and he brought out the best in everybody he played with. I certainly have a ton of respect and admiration for him."

Unlike several of his predecessors, Drew was setting records in the era of social media and cellphones, so on this big night, Archie's congratulatory text was one of many he received. That translated into lots of messages he would have to return.

"Well, I've got a hundred, probably two hundred on my phone right now to get to," he told me afterward. "You know this week was hard. I was just trying to lock in and focus, just stay in the moment. I'm gonna take some time this week to thank a lot of people."

It was impossible for Drew to personally thank all the 73,000 fans in attendance, but I brought up with him on such a monumental evening, a feeling that one day potentially 140,000 locals would claim to have attended such a historic New Orleans evening? I wondered how much that meant to him that many will say they were there even though they weren't because it was that big a night for the city and the franchise.

"Yeah, it does," he said. "The last 13 years, think about all the big moments that have occurred in this Dome, going back to Gleason's blocked punt, the reopening of the Dome on Monday Night Football in '06, so many great moments and then this Monday Night. Hopefully, we have quite a few left. I just enjoy these one at a time."

More would come, but this milestone was memorable on many levels. To put it into perspective, Brees' career passing yards equated to the following: over 41 miles, 184,000 po'boys, 317 Superdomes, 80 french quarters. I asked him, which one impressed him the most? "Po'boy one sounds cool. That's a lot of po'boys," Drew said.

It was also impressive that the Brees boys stayed close and well behaved for the entirety of my interview with Dad, so I thought we should reward them and have all three: Baylen, Bowen, and Callen, who were nine, seven, and five respectively at the time, join us. Drew agreed, and all three moved from behind the camera and perfectly lined up in front of their record-setting father. It became clear how much pride Drew took in sharing this moment with his sons, when I said to him, "To have them here, you can't beat this, can you?" Drew paused, smiled, and gently rubbed all of his boys' heads and said: "It's awesome. I think their favorite things is to play with (Saints Pro Bowl defensive lineman) Cam Jordan's son Tank, so basically they had their own football game going in the locker room."

Meanwhile, the Brees boys continued to soak in the moment too. They had fun watching themselves on camera through the nearby monitor and giving thumbs up or down to each other's appearances on television. Dad continued, "They were just tackling Tank, blocking for Tank. Of course, with a name like Tank, he's gonna either be a stud running back or a stud linebacker or something like that, yeah they had a good time."

Of course, Drew will remember the magical night more for his sons being with him, but it means a lot to him that they will retain much of it, too. After the interview, Dad gave his trio a group hug, kissed them all on the head, and exited stage right. It was way past their bedtime.

Passing Dan Marino (Single Season Yardage Record, December 29th, 2011)

Drew Brees always had an interesting relationship with the Miami Dolphins. Coming out of Purdue, he thought there was a good possibility they would draft him. Then the franchise infamously showed heavy interest when he reached free agency after leaving San Diego in 2006. As it is with Brees and the Saints, Dan Marino is usually the first name that comes to mind when you think of the Dolphins. In an era where quarterbacks didn't light up scoreboards as much as they do now, Marino was a clear exception, a notion prevalent with Drew, whose first NFL game was a pre-season game in South Florida in 2001.

"I remember walking in the stadium for the first time and looking up in the Ring of Honor and seeing Dan Marino's name and every passing record next to it," he remembered years later.

At that time, Drew was a rookie who just wanted to ensure he would be a backup with the Chargers, But looking up at Marino's name, he thought how unconscionable it would be for anyone to touch this seemingly elusive record.

"Just looking at those numbers is mind-boggling," he said. "You kind of say yourself, 'How long do you have to play in order to achieve something like that?'"

For Drew, the answer was eight seasons. In 2008, his third year in New Orleans, the Saints weren't going to the postseason, but the offense was humming and he entered the final game of that season at home versus Carolina needing 401 yards to catch Marino. It seemed attainable as he had thrown for over 420 yards in games versus Atlanta and Denver earlier in the year, but against the Panthers, he came up 15 yards short. Looking back after coming so close, Drew told me on this record-setting night that he had shared with his teammates during the week after the 2008 season he thought he would never have the chance to beat the record again. "I did think that, and the reason being, back in 08, we found ourselves in a lot of shootouts, a lot of come from behinds where we were throwing the ball a lot, a lot. There's a reason only one person has thrown for over 5000 yards, and it's Dan Marino, and that's why that was the record because it was a lot of yards."

After 2008 the Saints became a complete offense, earning more victories but fewer chances for Drew to catch Marino. Yet following this record-breaking night, he reflected with me on how the offense evolved from 2008 to that memorable night in December of 2011.

"When we got close to that, it was like, 'Ah, we'll never throw the ball enough to get to that point because we strive for balance,'" Drew told me. "But I don't think we thought we'd be averaging 450 plus yards per game either. Now we're in a position where, you know, as the season was going on, that was the last thing I was ever thinking about until maybe a few weeks ago when it became a real scenario where not only do we have a chance to break this but at the pace we're on, we may break it in week 15. And then you look on the calendar, and it's Monday Night Football against the Falcons, and you know what's at stake and you're just goin, 'Could that night get any bigger?'"

It was the first of many primetime record-breaking nights in the Superdome for the Saints quarterback, but it proved to be much more challenging than some other of his legendary games. On the surface, the record seemed more than attainable. After all, Drew had thrown for 300 or more yards 12 times already that season and he needed just 305 yards to break the record on this night. As fate would have it, though, the tempo of the game dictated a tough climb up Marino mountain. Drew and the Saints were 75 yards shy at the half, and the Falcons defense proved stingy, holding the Saints quarterback to 45 passing yards through the first 56 minutes of play. Plays like Darren Sproles' 92-yard kick return and Malcolm Jenkins' fumble recovery for a touchdown took opportunities away.

Afterward, I asked Drew if there were moments in the game where he may have been pressing, thinking about the record? He pointed to those plays and said, "So Sprolesy returns it down to the 15 or whatever, so I figure, 'Well we're not gonna break it now.' And then Jenkins picks up the fumble and scores, so 'We're not gonna break it now either.' All of these things kept happening, so I wasn't sure if we were going to get the opportunity again. You know, I felt like we had squandered an opportunity or two in the fourth quarter. You just hope to get the ball back, and then we get the ball back, and then we're wondering if it's enough field."

Unlike the 2008 season, when the clock ran out on his chase to Marino, Drew had a different mindset approaching the milestone this time, doing his best to block out any doubts about the record as time was ticking down late.

"So I really just tried to put it out of my mind and say, 'If it happens tonight, great; I still want to end this night on a good note, so let's sustain a drive, let's go down and try to score a TD.' I guess we accomplished it all at once, which was great."

Drew and the Saints waited till the last minute, or minutes, and with 2:51 left in the game and what would prove to be his final play of the night, he found his former Chargers and now current Saints teammate Sproles for the score and the record.

Ironically it was a 9-yard touchdown pass that sealed it for the Saints number 9. Afterward, I asked him how it sounds to be the NFL's all-time single-season yardage record holder?

"It sounds pretty significant," he said. "We've been talking about this for a long time. It seems like every week, I've really tried to downplay it, you know, compartmentalize it the best I can. Just think about winning, just think about executing the offense, being the best quarterback I can be out there, the best decision-maker."

Drew relished the moment but acknowledged the record was bigger than him.

"The fact we now as a team have broken that record, it's pretty phenomenal, the fashion that in which we did it too," he said. "I guess we made it pretty dramatic, so just try to enjoy the moment as much as we could and then in the locker room afterwards, 'This is a night that we'll never forget.'"

It was a magical and improbable night, and later that evening Drew shared with me that, even when he broke the mark, it came as a surprise.

"What's funny is, I felt like everybody on the sideline knew how close we were, maybe everybody in the stadium knew how close we were and yet, I didn't."

It was an unexpected yet happy ending for the Saints' record-breaker who broke a mark that had been standing since 1984. For perspective on how rare this feat was, only nine passers have eclipsed the 5000-yard milestone since Drew, including current Saints quarterback Jameis Winston, who did it with the Bucs in 2019. Peyton Manning broke his single season passing record in 2013 by remarkably throwing for one more passing yard than Drew threw in 2011.

While passing for over 5000 yards may be more common in today's game, the most revealing stat for the Saints quarterback is he's the only player to do it more than once. And he did it five times.

All-Time Touchdown King (December 17th, 2019)

Sometimes the NFL has it down to a science, and sometimes they get lucky. For years the NFL schedule makers slotted those New Orleans prime time games perfectly for Drew as he passed Marino, Unitas, and Manning, respectively. This record was different. In 2019, he was poised to pass Peyton Manning again, this time for most career touchdown passes. He entered the season needing 19, which was curious because the Saints' national games included the opener and a week four matchup versus the Cowboys. Neither would provide a showcase to break the record. The Saints were slotted to play the Falcons on Thanksgiving, which may have been the intended goal, but Drew missed five games due to a thumb injury. Ironically, that set the league up perfectly. Thanks to a big five-touchdown performance versus San Francisco in Week 14, he was only two touchdown passes shy of Manning, and what was on deck? Ironically a Monday Night game against Manning's former team, the Indianapolis Colts. The NFL had another golden primetime Brees moment on their hands, and in this instance, the plot would thicken as it was also the night the franchise celebrated the 10th anniversary of the Saints only Super Bowl victory. Amazingly only Drew and punter Thomas Morstead remained from that legendary squad, and the added significance of the upcoming event even went over the head of its protagonist. That week during our in-studio interviews, I asked Drew about the impeccable timing.

"I'll be honest with you," he said with a laugh. "I didn't put it all together until you just said that all the guys were coming back for this weekend. It's Monday Night Football and we're a couple of touchdowns away from breaking the all-time mark."

What proceeded to take place was nearly everything Drew could have imagined and much more. After two first-half touchdown passes, he easily could have broken Manning's mark in the first half, but a questionable pass interference call nullified his potential record-breaking score to Tre'Quan Smith. Drew didn't waste any time in the second half as he hit Saints tight end Josh Hill for the record. I asked him afterward was it a relief to get the record out of the way.

"Yeah, absolutely," he said. "It kind of drifts in your mind every now and then and, you're just like, 'Alright, stop it, next play, you're just trying to stay focused."

The unpredictability of the record could drive a lot of players crazy, but Drew seemed to be adjusting to anticipating the moment, knowing he couldn't force anything.

"You never know how it's gonna happen, when it's gonna happen or if it's gonna happen," he said. "Obviously, with lots of buildup and Monday Night Football and everybody's talking about it, you just try to stay laser-focused on each play one at a time, even as you get close to the end zone. It's just about putting the ball in the end zone however you can, doesn't matter if it's run or pass. If you get opportunities to make the plays, you make the plays."

Drew led his Saints to scoring drives in their first six possessions giving the home team the 34-0 lead, but that wasn't his most significant accomplishment. On such a momentous evening, he was almost perfect, completing 29 of 30 passes. His lone blemish was a 2nd quarter incompletion intended for running back Latavius Murray.

"That was unexpected," he said with a laugh. "I say all the time, 'The ball shouldn't touch the ground.' I prepare that way. I visualize that way."

Drew, for years would often agonize over the few blemishes on his stat sheet. This was no exception. The chance to go 30 for 30 and set the record was so close, but he put the incompletion to Murray on himself.

"My job as a quarterback is to be a great decision maker, and sometimes a great decision is to throw the ball away, right?" he said. "So typically, you have three or four of those a game and that combined with some defenders making some good plays you know whatever that might be you still hope to be really efficient. You're always thinking positive plays, moving the ball forward, getting first downs, scoring points. That's part of being efficient, it's a part of being a great decision-maker, so if you focus on that, the stuff takes care of itself"

Unlike other records, Drew knew immediately that remaining the all-time touchdown king would be difficult, if not impossible, what with another future Hall of Famer nipping at his heels. Tom Brady was only three behind him when the mark was set, so I asked him, "This is going to be interesting moving forward with you guys, isn't it?"

"He's such a stud," Drew told me of Brady. "I guess it brings out the best in both of us. I have so much respect for him, he's unbelievable."

Brady would ultimately take over the record during the 2020 season, but on the night that Drew broke the record, Brady showed his respect for him, when he tweeted, "Congrats, Drew!! Couldn't be more deserving. Passing Peyton in anything is an incredible achievement, and your record will be tough to beat. But it's worth trying (adding a winking emoji)."

Drew may have lost the record, but he passed Peyton Manning in fewer games than Brady and finished his career with an overall winning record against the ageless Patriots and Buccaneers quarterback.

Against Manning's former team, Drew defeated the Colts on a night where I wondered, "What's different about this record?"

Drew, in his last legendary milestone evening in the NFL, brought his collection of record-breaking evenings full circle, saying, "Think about the moments and how many of these transpired and came together. Monday Night Football for three of them, Sunday Night Football for one of them, I mean prime time games at home in front of our home fans, yeah you're trying to anticipate somewhat. Kudos to the NFL for their scheduling. Other than that, you just shake your head, I can't explain it, I can't explain it."

In his playing days, Drew would never answer my many questions on which record meant the most or would last the longest? He would always point to his career not being over, choosing to discuss those topics when he retired. When his playing days were over, I tried to revisit those subjects, but in true Brees fashion, he refused to play favorites regarding his records.

"I guess the good problem is that each happened in such a special way," Drew told me on his record-breaking night. "Most of the records as far as yardage and a few of the others didn't necessarily have to happen with touchdowns, but they did. Obviously, most touchdowns was gonna happen. Fifty-four consecutive touchdowns was gonna happen with a touchdown, but the all-time yardage record didn't have to happen with a touchdown, but did, with this crazy play to Tre'Quan Smith on Monday Night

Football. The single-season yardage record back in (2011) that didn't have to happen with a touchdown, but it did to Darren Sproles at the end of the game to kind of seal the deal against our arch-rival Falcons. It couldn't have been at a better moment."

In their entirety, Drew's records deservingly received a lot of attention on national TV, and each had a flair for the dramatic. But once his career was over, I gave it one last try asking which one was his favorite?

"I don't know," he said. "You clump all of them together, you really can't pick a favorite because each one has such a special meaning. Each one just kind of stands alone for what it represents."

Drew remained consistent, not playing favorites and never taking full credit for so many historic nights. What means the most to him is the overall impact smashing the modern-day record back meant to so many others.

"Each one covered such a long period of time that so many people were able to be a part of that and share in that and be the reason for that, so they're all special," he said.

6

Family Life

When fans think of the Brees family, for many the first image that comes to mind is Dad chasing his kids around after practice, a game or on the sideline at the Pro Bowl. Saints fans have also seen plenty of images of Dad coaching his three sons on flag football fields too. Ironically, the first image became the last image, too.

After Drew's final game in New Orleans against the Bucs in the 2020 playoffs and following an abnormal year when fans, for the most part, couldn't attend games due to COVID 19, the last glimpse of the Saints quarterback was on the Superdome turf playing football with his family. It was a Brees family tradition that the family didn't have a chance to enjoy all season.

"This year with COVID was tough because we obviously didn't have the same interaction with the fans like we normally do in the Superdome," Drew said, "and literally after every home game for the last four or five years, we've almost created this tradition where all the guys are bringing their kids down on the field. I'd say our team was pretty unique from the perspective, we had a lot of veteran guys and we'd all watched our families grow over the years."

Drew knew this game would be his last, so he made sure his family would be able to soak it in with Dad, who made it a point to make up for the lost time.

"We missed that this year," he said at season's end. "I felt like, 'Doggone it, my kids are gonna get an opportunity to do this one last time. We're gonna get out there, and we're gonna make them shut the lights out on us,' which they did about midnight."

I remember watching from the Superdome press box where it was impressive knowing it was the last game of his legendary NFL career, yet there was Drew with what had to be a million potential thoughts in his mind still focusing on his family. A family who had shared Dad with his busy career their whole lives. Drew understood the balance and sympathized with the toll it took on his children and his wife, Brittany.

"Literally, when training camp starts, you know that was my wife saying goodbye and realizing that is now a seven-month commitment that's coming up where we don't get a chance to see each other very much, and you don't get to see the kids very much," he said.

While the Brees boys have gained much media attention, the matriarch of Drew's household has always been pivotal. Before he was a father of four, his wife Brittany had a significant influence on him. His teammates concur.

"Brittany made him grow up quick," Flutie said.

The Flutie and Brees families remain close, but the veteran saw early on how much Brittany meant to his protégé.

"I'd say, 'What's goin on Drew? What are you doing?,'" Flutie said. "And he'd say, I'm going to a wine tasting.' I was like, 'Wine tasting?' So he came around in a hurry. All of a sudden, he's wearing suits and dressed up and mature. I still haven't matured. I'm a hundred years old, I'm still playing baseball, I have a hockey game tonight."

Drew and Brittany met at Purdue, always dreaming of raising a family wherever Brees' football destination would take them. It just happened to be in New Orleans, where the couple has raised millions through the Brees Dream Foundation to uplift the community and backup their mission statement, which is to continue to improve the quality of life for cancer patients and provide the care, education, and opportunities for children and families in need. The Foundation has made an enormous impact on the New Orleans community after Katrina and most recently during the COVID-19 pandemic.

As their kids grew, so did the burden on Drew of being away from Brittany and their children. Many remember his oldest son Baylen, whom Drew famously held when he was just a baby boy on the Super Bowl stage. Times had changed.

"My son Baylen is gonna be in seventh grade next year," Brees said at the end of the 2020 season. "You begin to think about those other priorities in your life. My time with my wife and my family is so valuable and so important. It's finite from the perspective that once (the kids) leave the roost, there's only this finite amount of time that you have them in your house. I was ready to move on. I was ready for the next chapter in my life."

Time will tell how much his kids will remember running around the Superdome after Dad's last game, but for Brees, it was always important that he played long enough that his kids would have some memories of his playing days. I asked him back in 2014 how nice it would be to pattern his career with his family in the fashion Archie Manning did with his sons, to have them around long enough so that they would remember being a part of it?

"That factors into it, it really does because their enthusiasm for the game and watching Daddy play on Sunday and knowing who players are, and wanting to wear their jerseys and run around the house and play tackle football with Daddy, that's awesome," Drew told me. "There are not many better feelings as a father than just having those moments with your kids."

This mindset was evident not only after his last game but throughout his whole career. The Saints quarterback made it a priority to keep his family omnipresent.

The 2018 Pro Bowl was a great example.

Drew's mindset was to make sure his sons would enjoy the entire experience. It seemed like fate as the Brees boys caught a break as school was canceled all week due to freezing weather conditions in New Orleans. Dad took advantage and set the tone by having all three sons write a letter to Sean Payton, who served as the NFC's Head Coach, asking to become official ball boys. Each note was handwritten and for good measure was complemented with several Sour Patch Kids candies to gain more favor with the Head Saint. After a formal interview, Payton quickly made it official on Twitter: "Baylen, Bowen, and Callen crushed the interview today! They will be joining the NFC team at the Pro Bowl. Congrats Boys!"

After the family arrived in Orlando, I had a chance to witness the drama unfold. It was impressive seeing Drew have one eye on his job as NFC quarterback and the other on the whereabouts of the Brees boys on the practice field. It was just what he had envisioned when they were born, bringing them to work, having them absorb what Dad does and ultimately creating memories they will hopefully never forget.

"This is what it's all about," Drew told me after the first Pro Bowl practice, his boys all pulling at him during the interview. "You never know when you'll get a chance to come back and be a part of something like this, so it's cool to have them involved."

Payton gave the boys high marks for their job performance, despite the fact there were a few glitches." They did good," Payton said. "We had a little shoe problem with one of them, but we had that corrected and got the water squared away. Overall, I'd say it was a pretty good first day."

It was an experience that was unfolding every bit the way Drew envisioned as his teammates were as accepting to his kids as Payton was.

"They got to be on their 'A' game at all times." Saints running back and NFC Pro Bowler Alvin Kamara said. "Drew tells them to (move the ball) you got to put the laces up. Yeah, their doin their job. They're handling it."

The proud papa agreed.

"When the guys needed some water, (they) got them water, and the rest of the time (they) just goofed around and played football," he said. The Brees boys were enjoying every moment but playfully disagreed with Dad that they goofed around on this day. It was clear they relished being a part of their father's practice and wanted his approval.

"They did a great job today spotting the balls for the guys, getting the water, doing whatever they're asked to do," Drew acknowledged.

Part of their Pro Bowl responsibility was to stay out of the way and not to get into it with each other. The latter goal was more challenging than the former, as anyone who watched the 2018 Pro Bowl on TV will likely remember. The cameras captured many shots of the Brees boys wrestling with each other on the sidelines. The crew earned valuable TV time wrestling in the background while Dad was doing an interview on the sideline during the game. Drew played quarterback first and referee second.

"That was the game within the game," Drew told me afterward. "It was like a WWE wrestling match on the sidelines. They had more chalk all over them and hit the ground more than everybody out there combined."

Yes, in a game not known for its physicality, the Brees boys made up for it. If it wasn't Baylen tackling Bowen, it was Callen tackling Baylen or sometimes Bowen tackling Callen. The boys put on an entertaining sideshow, one which their parents, Drew and Brittany, saw coming a mile away.

But like any good football team, Mom and Dad implemented their own Pro Bowl game plan.

"I told my wife, you take them to the stands while I'm playing, so I can focus and concentrate on the game, and once I'm done, I'll come over and get em," Drew explained. "By the time it's pouring down rain, they came down with ponchos. It was on and off throughout the game, but they loved every second."

Once the rain subsided and the Brees boys settled in, I asked Dad how special the week had been for him. "Yeah, no doubt, it's made the week," he said. "It's awesome being with the guys in the locker room, but to have them be a part of everything, every practice to every rep to the game, they had such a good time."

Drew always got a kick out of how his son's favorite players were routinely someone other than him. Like Archie Manning, who used to laugh over how his boys favored Dallas Cowboys Hall of Fame quarterback Roger Staubach over him, Drew could only smile at the thought of how his sons preferred stars such as Odell Beckham Jr. A big reason was the Giants receiver went to the same school as they did, Isidore Newman in New Orleans.

"They know all these players," Drew reasoned. "That's the crazy thing. They see a guy walk by and they say, 'Hey, that's Jalen Ramsey,' or 'That's so and so.' It's crazy just to see what big fans they are and how they truly know the players."

I remember asking Drew how his family life would change now that another season was coming to a close?

"I'll just relax with the family, spend a lot of time with them, start helping out with the kids' homework again and all the stuff I missed out on during the season," he said. "Just a ton of family time."

By then, time had become more precious for Drew. When we first met, he didn't have any kids, which was the case in his first three seasons in New Orleans. Then, as his stardom rose, his family grew. First came Baylen, then Bowen, then Callen. Finally, their only daughter, Rylen, was born. With each addition to the Brees depth chart, Drew's fame and notoriety increased to the point where he became a future Hall of Famer as well as a proud Dad of four. As it did, the time that used to be all his own was devoted to his family. That, too, required an adjustment.

"I think everybody looks back and asks themselves, 'What did we do with all that free time (before kids),'" Drew told me in 2017. "So, for, me, I have a routine now, literally every 10-to-15-minute block throughout the day is laid out so I know exactly what I'm doing or supposed to be doing."

Drew knew that juggling family matters would require more than just a few adjustments, but in the process, it made him more sufficient with his time.

"I think it maximized my efficiency and my focus," he said. "I know, for example, that I have to get my studying done in the next 30 minutes, because I want to go home and read a book to my kids before they go to bed."

It wasn't easy, but for this Dad, it was more than worth the extra effort.

"That's what fills my bucket up," he said. "That's what I need for the balance of my time with my life or whatever that may be."

The Saints quarterback thrived on his routine as a football player with a focus that took his game to a whole new level in New Orleans. Putting the same effort into his family schedule gave him the chance to be the kind of Dad he had always envisioned himself being.

"I just know I have to be laser-focused, so I can be present when I'm with my kids or present with what I'm doing again in the moment," he said. "I want to be in the moment. I want that to have all of my attention, so that

I don't have to think back and say, 'I should have made better use of that time.' I can't afford that. I gotta be locked in."

With a growing family, Drew had to have greater focus during our interviews, especially during the chaotic 2020 season. Unlike past years, the coronavirus prohibited us from meeting face to face, so we had to conduct our post-game shows via the newfound Zoom technology. I didn't know what to make of this dynamic at first but grew to like how different it was as we both made the best of it. It was evident during the four games where Drew sat out for the second straight season due to injury. Unlike the thumb injury in 2019, the injury he suffered a year later was much more severe as he endured an incredible 11 broken ribs as well as a punctured lung. But you never sensed how bad it was during the stretch he was out, as Drew always appeared the same on camera. His constant juggling of football and family came into focus in one of our most memorable interviews from the Brees homestead in that final season.

After his first game out when the passing and running of Taysom Hill led the Saints to a 24-9 drubbing of the Falcons, I initially thought Drew would join us from his usual spot outside the Saints locker room in the Superdome. Instead, he opted to do our interview from home. I wasn't sure how this would work as we had never attempted it before? When he logged on to our Zoom call, there was Drew ready to go inside his kitchen.

I asked him, "Is this where we are gonna do it?"

He replied, "This isn't ok?"

Before I had a chance to say it was, Drew, ever the perfectionist, quickly found a better location in the family living room with a better background. It was classic Brees.

What ensued was also classic Brees, only on a family scale as he never once would flinch during our seven-minute interview despite the myriad of household distractions around him. During our interview, you could hear his wife Brittany tell the kids to "be quiet, Daddy's doing an interview" and the faint noises of the boys playing in the background. Then at the end of our interview, as if it was planned, the family dog landed in his lap. It was must-see Zoom TV.

During this Brees family exclusive, I asked Drew how much the injury altered his day-to-day routine?

"The kids can't jump on me like they normally do when I walk in the door," he said.

The injury also interrupted Dad's daily routine with the kiddos.

"So much of what we do, like every day for at least 20-to-35-to-45 minutes, is throwing the ball around," he said. "Whether it's on the trampoline or just goofing around in the living room, or the park, or something like that. So, no throwing for a bit."

This zoom interview offered insight into Drew's life that we never would have predicted when we first proposed the idea to his camp before the season. For example: "I can still play barbies, I can still paint fingernails for my daughter, we're being creative," he said.

For years, it looked as if Brittany would be the only female in the house. That all changed in August 2014 when Rylen Judith Brees was born. A year later, I remember asking Drew how Rylen altered the family dynamic.

"Before the little girl, when it was just the boys, I'd walk in the house, and it was immediately to the boys, and we were just wrestling and just doing boy stuff, but it was immediately right into the action," Drew said.

As he continued the interview, his expression changed as he described his only daughter and her impact on him and the family.

"But now, I give everybody a kiss and a hug, but that little girl comes up to me it's now da da da da da, and she wants me to pick her up, and she will not let me put her down for at least an hour," Drew said. "So, whatever

I do now, I'm doing it with her kind of attached to a shoulder. So if it's wrestling with the boys and I'm wrestling, I got her the whole time, and I might throw her in the mix a little bit, and then I got her again. She will not let me put her down, so it's a lot of daddy-daughter time, which is fantastic."

It's clear Rylen is a Daddy's girl. But she's not afraid to put him in his place when the time is right.

"She's something else," he marveled. "She loves being in the mix with her brothers at times. On other occasions, it's like, 'Dad it's time for you to spend time with me, and me alone.' It's gotta be daddy-daughter time alone, and 'Boys, you do your thing, it's daddy-daughter time.'"

My favorite memory of Rylen Brees was after a Saints road game in Dallas, Texas, Drew's home state. On this night, predictably, he had a lot of family waiting for him outside the locker room, including all of his kids. While his boys were playing with each other, I remember looking off to the side and seeing Rylen methodically and routinely pull off perfect cartwheel after cartwheel. It was impressive. A few weeks later, I asked Drew about what I saw, and he delivered a great story of the origination of Rylen's gymnastic talents.

"Yeah, it's pretty strong, "he said. "In fact, that morning, Brittany took the kids to a museum in Dallas which had a computer screen of several elite athletes, and they're doing different things. You do something in front of a green screen, and they match you up alongside the professional, and so they had a professional gymnast doing a cartwheel. So, Rylen did her cartwheel, and they matched it up (against the professional image), and it was identical. It was actually freaky identical. Made me proud."

After the proud papa told that story, the competitor in him came out a bit.

"I don't think she got any of that cartwheel ability from me," Brees said smiling. "I think that came from Mom. But I'm gonna take a little bit of credit."

So, look out, maybe we'll see Rylen Brees represent the United States gymnastics team in the summer games of 2034?

With kids of my own, Drew and I often compared things such as the Halloween costumes our children wore over the years. His kids evolved from dressing up as superheros to a phase where they wanted to be various Star Wars characters and eventually their favorite football players. We also were able to take several peeks into what the Brees household was like during the holidays, especially during the 2020 season when the Saints had to play on Christmas Day for the first time in franchise history. It presented a tricky dynamic for many players, including their quarterback, who had to juggle Santa's arrival with the upcoming game versus Minnesota.

Through the power of Zoom, Drew shared with me on Christmas Day 2020 how he pulled off being both Dad, Santa and Saints quarterback. In our interview after the Vikings game, I assumed Christmas was just getting started at the Brees household, so I asked him how the game affected the holiday with his family?

"We'll have Christmas when I get home, so I've been looking forward to this moment," he said. "This will be awesome. Short week, you're trying to cram preparation. Last night I didn't get home until late 6:30. I only have like an hour before I have to head to the team hotel and kind of get ready."

He continued the story, saying that when he got home, his family had a surprise in store.

"Literally, as I'm walking into the door, the latch opens, and two of my boys throw Christmas pajamas in my arms and say, 'Hurry, go get dressed,' because normally on Christmas morning, the kids would come wake Brittney and I up, early early. And we would tell them to go back to bed, it's not time yet, then finally get up and sit on the steps and do a family picture. So we had to do that last night because obviously, I couldn't be there this morning. So we did the family picture last night in Christmas pajamas, and we let the kids open up a few gifts last night, mainly like from grandma and people who had sent stuff. They got to open up a few Santa gifts this morning, and they'll get to open up the remainder when I get home."

It was a day of audibles on and off the field for Drew, who delivered his detailed Christmas Day breakdown. My first thoughts were to credit his kids for being so patient with all the unusual holiday distractions. Instead, Drew gave me a candid response every parent could fully appreciate.

"They're definitely not patient," he said. "They weren't willing participants in withholding some gifts from them. They wanted to just rip open all the bags at once."

Like any family, sharing holiday memories stands out, but when many think of Drew Brees and his family, the memory which often is front and center came from his decision to have his then one-year-old son Baylen in his arms on the podium when the Saints won their first Super Bowl. Brittany was ready for the moment supplying baby Baylen with headphones. It was a picture-perfect moment, iconic, something new to a celebration of that magnitude. It endeared many whom didn't know much about the Saints quarterback. It also shed light on how much his family meant to him.

In 2014, when Baylen was five, I asked Brees about that moment. Does Baylen better appreciate it now, I asked? How often does he talk about it?

"We've seen it a few times, but haven't seen it in a long time," he said. "He'll see the Sports Illustrated cover, or there's trading cards with that image on it. I actually have a big picture in my office of it. He'll make comments every now and then. Really, it's his brothers who say, 'That's Bay Bay.' Callen is the real talker now, he just turned two," Drew told me in 2014. " Whenever I see it, they will absolutely point anything football-related right now. They're into it."

2009 was quite a year for the father and his oldest son. Baylen who was born on the same day as Drew and just over a year later both created a memory that will live in Super Bowl lore. "I think long term that will be one of the most special moments for the both of us," Drew said.

These days, Drew and his boys are making new memories on the flag football field. While Drew enjoys actively coaching his boys, he told me years before they could participate what his mindset concerning their participation would eventually be.

"I will absolutely let my boys play football, tackle football, but waiting until they are an appropriate age is something I will absolutely do," he said. "I think there are so many other ways to enjoy the sport of football without putting pads on at 7, 8, or 9."

It was the same plan Drew's parents had for him

"I played flag football sixth, seventh and eighth grade," he said. "I didn't put pads on until ninth grade, and for a lot of guys in my locker room, it was the same way. There's dangers, there's risk of injury in every sport, just at different levels."

While many parents justifiably worry about the growing number of concussions stemming from tackle football, Drew worries too. But he puts his sport in perspective.

"What I found interesting is the second-highest concussions rate behind football is women's soccer, so who would have thought?" he asked rhetorically. "The key is understanding the risk of injury with each sport and knowing once an injury does occur how to treat it and make sure everything is all good once your child steps back on the field again. Injuries come with the territory. When it comes to sports, certainly that has become a big topic with the NFL, and rightfully so."

Even though he's the ultimate competitor, I never pictured Drew yelling and screaming at his kids, the officials, or opposing parents, but I asked him before his kids played competitively, what kind of Dad would he be watching his kids play sports? His response at the time was, as usual, measured, as if he had put a lot of thought into it.

"I feel like I've experienced it at a small level, watching cousins, nephews and that kind of thing play and just visualizing what this will be like as a parent (because) you have somewhat of a vested interest," he said. "You are observing other parents."

At the time, Drew looked forward to the possibility of one day watching his children compete and knew that experiencing the rigors of the NFL would only assist him in the process of parenting his kids.

"I have an interesting perspective based upon the fact I've played professional sports for a living," he said. "You gotta take your hands off the wheel and just let your kids play. I think the biggest element to youth sports is letting your kids have fun. They have the rest of their life to bear down and focus. Certainly, you don't want to narrow down a sport for a child until it's absolutely necessary."

Drew wants his kids to follow whatever passion they desire but doesn't shy away from seeing the advantages that competition would one day bring.

"I'm going to encourage them to play sports," he said. "I'm going to encourage them to play as many sports as they want to and can handle. The expectation is when you step on the field, you are giving it 100 percent, you are not gonna quit, and there's all these life lessons that are gonna come up through sports."

Drew had put a lot of thought into his role with his kids in athletics and anticipated how he would handle the hard times, years before his kids started actively competing.

"Are they gonna come up to me crying because they hit their shin with somebody on the soccer field? Probably. Are they gonna cry if they get pulled out of the game, lost or struck out? Yes, that's gonna happen. You know what, those are good things because life lessons can come from that, so I'm waiting for those moments to be able to instill those life lessons into them based upon sports, and that's what's so great about youth sports."

Drew is getting the chance to live the life he envisioned with his growing family these days. His passion for football mirrors the pride he takes in being a great Dad. It's sincere and often on display in his Saints career, a love he shared with many of his teammates.

"We all encounter different chapters in our lives, right?" he said. "I've had this football chapter for a while, but I feel along with that has come these different phases of having no kids to having one child, to now having four children, and it's fun to see my friends and former teammates also going through that as well. In many cases, a lot of our kids are the same ages, so you have a lot of similar conversations, similar challenges, talking about your kids."

For the Saints quarterback, leaving the game was tough on many levels. He knew he would miss his teammates, miss the competition, but Drew also knew that stepping away from football would, to some degree, take something equally special away from his kids, too. That was evident when I interviewed Drew in the Superdome right after his last game and moments before he played with his children on the Superdome turf for the final time as an active player.

"A part of me feels that when I do leave the game, I'll be taking a little bit of that element away from them, too," he said. "The experience of going to the facility and running around and talking about it in the house, taking them to the Superdome and daddy's on the field. All those feelings man, those are great feelings. We're building some pretty awesome memories right now, and I'd like for that to be able to last us as long as we can."

7

Behind The Scenes

So, what is Drew Brees like behind closed doors, inside the locker room, away from the media and the fans? Few can answer those questions better than those who worked with him in those spaces every day.

"He is top-notch for us," said Blake Romig, a veteran member of the Saints equipment staff from 2014 to 2020. "We see him every morning. He treats us with respect, always asks how we're doing, things like that."

Romig can attest to Brees being respectful to his crew even when he doesn't respect his gear. "When he has a bad throw at practice, he gets pissed, and a lot of times he'll slam his helmet, and part of our job is if a helmet breaks or an earpiece pops out, you want to grab the helmet and fix it real quick and give it back to him," Romig said. "But with Brees, it's the complete opposite. He doesn't want you to grab his helmet because they'll be a time, he overthrows the ball, he'll slam his helmet, earpiece pops out. When that happens, (my mindset is) 'I gotta go, I gotta go,' but he'll put his helmet back on without the earpiece, and he's yelled at a few guys like, 'Don't grab my helmet, don't touch my helmet. I'll fix it. I made the mistake, I'll fix it,' which is kind of respect-worthy."

The Saints support staff appreciates Drew's respect even in small areas such as his helmet on the practice field. It was refreshing to see the team's franchise quarterback prioritizing not making their jobs harder, a notion which took a while for Romig to get used to. "I remember early on, I ran over there and tried to fix (his helmet), but my boss grabbed me and said, 'No, no, no, don't touch it. I'm saving you from getting yelled at. It turned into a known thing. Don't look into his eyes when he throws (his helmet), and don't grab his helmet."

Drew's helmet isn't to be touched, but that doesn't mean it can't be the source of jokes. Entering the 2015 season, the Saints quarterback was pondering switching his helmet to a bigger and safer model, but it didn't receive rave reviews in his huddle, especially from one of his favorite targets, receiver Lance Moore.

"I put that thing on, and I remember Lance's face when I walked into the huddle." Drew said. "He just kind of stood up and looked at me and said, 'Bro, I cannot take you serious wearing that helmet.'"

Moore remembers the episode with Drew vividly.

"That one sticks out to me for sure - Big Helmet Brees," Moore recalled. "Those big "Space Balls"-looking helmets came out that they're trying to mandate that everyone wears, I'm old school and I don't like them. I would have never worn them, so (Brees) jumps in the huddle, and I'm like, 'Hold on, hold on,' and this was (during) a team period (in practice), so the full huddle is here, the coaches are waiting for us, and I'm like, 'Hold on.' Everyone else (in the huddle) is like, 'Huh' and Drew is like, 'What?' I had to say something cause I was like, 'No, not you, Drew. You look, goofy man. You look terrible', and sure enough, by the end of that practice, he had the equipment managers run (into the locker room) and get his old helmet back. I said, 'That is the Drew Brees that I know and love.'"

"I was like, 'Listen, if my receiver, my guy, can't take me serious, if I don't have authority in the huddle wearing this martian-looking helmet, then this thing needs to go,'" Drew smiled looking back. "So, I put the old school helmet back on."

"He took it all in stride," Moore said. "He laughed just like everybody else. It was probably funnier for me because I was the one giving it to him, definitely just the sense of humor that he has. He took it in stride and enjoyed it too."

Drew eventually had to replace his outdated helmet because of safety concerns. That change took place in 2019.

"Out of 72 graded helmets, my old helmet was ranked second to last in safety," Drew remembered. "It was obsolete. They didn't make it anymore, and they basically banned it from use, but that was the helmet I played with for most of my career."

Many within the organization appreciate Drew's accountability and his ability behind the scenes to communicate to them respectfully what he needs. The staff has many responsibilities, including snapping the quarterbacks the ball during practice. The team labels these drills as pre-practice "routes on air," where the equipment crew fills in for the offensive lineman. It's a job where the support staff must be in total sync with Drew.

"My first time snapping with him, I was scared to death because you don't want to break his finger," Blake Romig said. "Once that happens, you're done, and he's probably out for a few weeks."

Blake's first big opportunity with Drew was during a game week. Admittedly nervous, he was fumbling the ball, just hoping not to make a mistake, but the Saints quarterback quickly calmed him down with some constructive criticism.

"Right after that period, Brees came up and said, 'Blake, you need to be more firm. You need to be quicker.' He was always saying, 'Expect the snap, be ready always, always anticipate it.' So then, I felt comfortable doing it. I could do it in my sleep, hopefully. But (I) still get a little scared doing it."

Drew isn't demanding but he did have a few gameday requests from his equipment guys.

"Eye black in his locker every game, and it's the old school eye black that they don't really sell anymore," Blake recalled. "He likes the used old-school eye black. Sometimes you have guys, they'll come up and ask you to put eye black under their eyes. Brees would do it himself, and usually, it was me putting it in his locker, and he always left it in the bathroom. Every game wherever we're at, he left it in the bathroom. The last few years, they stopped selling the eye black, so I remember my boss always saying, 'Hey, make sure you get that eye black back. We need that one back.' I don't even know the brand. The brand was marked off. It was a no-brand thing."

Drew always needed a particular eye black and requested a small-medium ballcap in his locker and one under the bench where he sat during the game. In return, Drew always made sure his crew was taken care of during the holidays.

"He is the best," Blake said. "He treats us well during the holidays. He's really a leader during Christmas time, helping and treating us well, rounding up players to help us out. He's awesome for us, probably one of the best players. Definitely a ringleader for that."

The Saints quarterback is also giving to his teammates behind closed doors. While many quarterbacks around the NFL deliver holiday gifts to their offensive lineman, Drew is no exception and is known for being creative and ridiculously generous with his yearly holiday presents.

"The Christmas gifts were always extravagant and unnecessary," Strief said. "You could see there was thought put into it each year. And you could always count on it being something exceptional and something you probably wouldn't get yourself. It was always something like very top of the line watches that I would never purchase. You know, special edition watches that we couldn't get if we wanted them. Everything was always very thoughtful."

It was tough for Strief to choose his favorite gift from Drew, but he admits a highlight was a trip he gave all of his linemen one season.

"The trips he gave us were always to amazing places," Strief said, "You get a bunch of options, first-class airfare. My first vacation with my wife was one of those trips."

Drew would dish out great gifts and plenty of his time when it came to his offensive linemen. The linemen met each Thursday during the season for their weekly dinner, and he always wanted to be a part of it. Even though he was often late because of extra film study, he would have Strief take a picture of the menu so he could order ahead. His protectors valued his participation each week.

"The fact that he made an effort to come, you're talking about a guy whose schedule during the football season starts at 6 a.m. or sometimes 5:30 a.m., whenever he got in the building each day and went until 7 or 7:30 at night," Strief said. "For him on a Thursday, a guy with children and a wife who's already committing more time than all of us to make an effort to come out and eat dinner? For him to make that effort, it always stuck with me. It was just the sacrifice. He saw the importance and valued the camaraderie. He enjoyed it. It was a release for him, too."

The Saints quarterback enjoyed eating with his lineman and occasionally picked up culinary advice from his teammates. In a pregame meal, he acquired a lifelong tip from one of his favorite wide receivers.

"One game we were eating pregame dinner together, and I had a chicken breast, and I put A1 sauce and honey all over it, "Lance Moore said. "(Brees) was like, 'What are you doing?' I said, 'I don't know, I've been doing this since college. Our chicken was terrible at (the University of)

Toledo, so we had to doctor it up, and I started doing this honey and A1 sauce thing.' It was amazing, so he started doing it. He said, 'I gotta keep doing this. It's so good.'"

"I totally thieved his little chicken pregame recipe there with the A1 and the honey," Drew admitted to me. "I still do it to this day. I did it ever since that moment, and I think we went out and balled that day, too. I think it was in Atlanta, went out and balled and had a big win, and I was like, 'I gotta keep this going now, and so I thieved that. Thank you, Lance."

One of the great privileges of interviewing Drew after every game for most of his career was seeing things many didn't see. Ironically, what I saw was what many knew as he is the same guy behind the camera as he is when the spotlight is bearing down on him. On countless occasions, whether it was after a win or a loss, I saw him wrap up his post-game duties and then pose for a picture with a fan or sign an autograph or two.

After doing so many interviews together, we agreed it was good to keep things "fresh" as I constantly broached new topics about his life on and off the football field. Drew can roll with anything, but now and then, we'd have fun playing a joke on a friend or a co-worker of mine. For years a videographer I worked with who went by the name of "Double D" loved to tease me and say, "Brees hates you." Double D would say it every time I'd see him. So, in one of our in-studio interviews, I decided to get my revenge.

I didn't brief Drew, but it was around Christmas, so I did a video saying on camera, "Merry Christmas Double D, it's the holiday season, so I wanted to clear the air. For years you have been saying Drew Brees hates me. Well, I happen to have Drew Brees right here, so let's ask him? Drew, you don't hate me, do you?"

His response was dead on. In an awkward, slightly drawn-out manner that included a brief pause, Drew said, "No, I don't hate you."

I replied, "you paused there?"

Drew countered, "Well, I had to think about it."

It was all right on cue. Then, in closing out the gag, Drew adlibbed the perfect exclamation point to end the video, saying, "Merry Christmas Double D." It was good to get that fun side out of him every once in a while.

Back in 2001, Eric Richey, a veteran sportscaster who covered Drew for years at Purdue and later in New Orleans, found out he loved the popular Ace Ventura movie and asked if he could deliver a Jim Carrey impression at his post-draft press conference at Purdue. Back then, Drew showed off his skills by nailing Carrey's signature line "Alrighty then" on the spot.

Number 9 has many layers. His quick-wit is one of them. We had a light segment called "More Likely" in which I would ask him three hypothetical questions involving a variety of topics ranging from football and his teammates to movies, music or his favorite TV show. It became a challenge to stump Drew, as he was quick even though he never knew what questions I was about to throw at him.

During the 2018 season, when Taysom Hill's popularity was rising and the competition inside the quarterback room was at a high-octane pace, I asked Drew if he was "More Likely" to beat Taysom in a game of horse, ping pong or tennis?

"I've seen him play horse," Drew said. "We got a little hoop in the locker room. He's pretty good, although I haven't played in a long time. Tennis is something I've never seen him play, but I know what I can do, so I'm gonna say tennis."

To get a feel for the comfort level of his Saints teammates, I asked Drew the same year if he had to drive from his driveway in New Orleans to San Diego with one of his teammates, which one would he choose to ride shotgun, Mark Ingram, Alvin Kamara, or Michael Thomas? Without hesitation, as if it was a no-brainer, Drew said, "Mark Ingram. I love all those guys, but Mark would keep me so entertained the entire time, regardless of the topic. We could just sit there and go karaoke on the radio, and I'd be entertained for all 27 hours. I could learn a lot from him. He could learn from me. It would be a good match."

I knew who was on Drew's short list of sports role models, so I put that knowledge to the test once, asking Drew if he could trade places with one of his favorite athletes growing up, which career would he take, Ted Williams', Nolan Ryan's, or Roger Federer's?

"The obvious choice would be Ted Williams," he said, "not only because of the baseball career but because the guy was probably one of the best fishermen. Like, the stuff he caught, how he caught it, where he caught it, pretty unbelievable. You know he logged all of his fishing trips in a journal (where he kept track of) who he fished with, where he was fishing, what fly he was using. It was unbelievable. Nolan Ryan pitched for 27 years professionally, and Federer is one of the most consistent, if not the most consistent tennis players. So, I'm gonna go with my guy Ted, who was a fighter pilot as well. I'd love to know what (it) was like sitting (in the cockpit) of an F9F fighter panther jet."

Drew's response didn't surprise me. After all, Williams wore number 9, and that's why he wore that number throughout his career. As much respect as Drew has for Ryan and as great as his passion for tennis is, Williams will always be his top sports role model. It's been that way since his younger years in Austin, where Drew enjoyed reading Williams' biography at a very young age.

During the 2017 season, I mixed up the questions even more and asked Drew if he was stranded on a deserted island for a month, which current Saints teammate would he choose to join him?

"I'm gonna say Max Unger," Drew said of the Saints starting center at the time. "And I'll tell you why: Max Unger grew up on the big island of Hawaii, grew up on a farm, a ranch, so I feel like he's really resourceful. He knows how to build things, (knows) agriculture and livestock, so we could build a good shelter, figure out how to grow some stuff, just survive. You would (acquire) some good survival skills."

Once again, I couldn't stump this guy. I never stopped trying, though, and once asked Drew if he could pick a Saints teammate past or present to star on Jeopardy, who would it be?

"The first guy that comes to mind is Strief," Drew quickly countered. "He's a Northwestern grad, which is just kind of a step below Purdue. (He's) been around a long time, pretty wise, well-read, knows a lot about a lot of things, I'm gonna go with Strief."

Ok, but I surely thought I would get him on my final question. So, here goes: you have four kids in a growing family, so which current or past teammate would you choose to be a babysitter for a night? Without hesitation, Drew offered up this:

"I'm gonna go with the wide receiver corps, my current wide receiver corps," he said.

I followed up, "It takes that many babysitters?" "It would take that many, yes, but (the kids) all have their jerseys, so what they would do is basically put them on, and these are the only guys that would have enough energy to run around and keep up with the four of them. So, I'm going with the wide receiver corps. And they're fast enough to catch them, yes."

Further proof, Drew trusted his wideouts.

His excellent relationship with Taysom Hill was evident in a collection of "More Likely" questions I asked him during the 2019 season. Hill had earned his swiss army knife status by doing everything on the football field by then, so I wondered how envious Drew was, asking him, "Will you ever catch a pass from Taysom?" Drew liked the possibility.

"I'm pushing for that," he said. "I don't know if that will ever happen.

It's probably not very likely to happen, but you never know. When you have to pull out all the stops, it's like ambush (referring to Payton's call in the Super Bowl to begin the second half with an unprecedented onside kick against the Colts).

I followed up, "But there's a chance?" Drew replied, "So you're saying there's a chance, there's always a chance," quoting the famous line from another Jim Carrey movie, Dumb and Dumber.

During the same interview, I asked, "Now that Max Unger has retired, who would be the best Saints teammate to have with you on a deserted island?"

"I'd probably choose Taysom Hill," Drew said. "Grew up in Idaho, grew up hunting. He was used to going out with his Dad and family on these week-long treks, where you're tracking elk and shooting them with a bow and arrow, cleaning them right there in the field and having meat. I just saw him on an advertisement for Idaho potatoes, so he's got to have some kind of agricultural background, too. So, we're talking survival, and he's a fun guy to be around, I'm thinking that's a good combination."

I noted, "You'll have the swiss army knife on the stranded island. "Bingo," Drew replied.

I had heard that Drew, even though he went to high school and college primarily in the '90s, was a big fan of 80's music. Drew loved the old-school one-hit wonders, so he answered more questions in a rapid-fire response type mode during one interview session. After acknowledging he loved the 80's playlists, I asked if there was a song or a band from the '80s that stuck out the most to him?

"What I am is like '80s on 8, XM Satellite Radio, and you're gonna hear 90's one-hit wonders," he said. "I don't know if there's like a number one."

Doing my job, I had to dig deeper, so I suggested, "something like "The Knack's My Sharona"?

Without skipping a beat, Drew dove in with a group of his favorite 80's hit songs, "You got 867-5309 Jenny (Tommy Tutone), all those, they're good. A little Whitesnake, Billy Idol, Billy Squier, there you go," I told him; "The Billy Squier reference is impressive." Drew laughed, proud he pulled the 80's star seemingly out of his back pocket.

Continuing to mix it up, I asked Drew, "You're one of the most famous Drew's on the planet, but give me your favorite Drew. Is it Drew Barrymore or Drew Carey?

Brees countered, "Drew Carey's funny, but I like Drew Barrymore, going back to the ET Days." Yet another 80's reference.

No matter how challenging I made the questions, I still couldn't stump the Saints quarterback.

"You wear number 9, right," I asked?

"Yes," Drew said wondering what was coming next.

"OK, if you could have nine of anything, what would you want," I pondered?

Again, without any stoppage in play, Drew came up with an answer that summarized his mindset as a player, saying, "nine more years to play in this league."

Ironically, I asked that question in 2013 where who would have thought Drew would almost play nine more seasons, just falling a few short.

In 2019, I revisited the same question: if number nine could have nine of anything, what would it be this time? I knew at this point in his career, he couldn't say nine more years. As usual, another quick response was fitting, considering his Saints were continually knocking on the door in terms of chasing Super Bowls.

"How about nine Super Bowl rings," Drew said. "It's not so much the ring. It's what it represents. It's the memories. It's the experiences, which I feel in my 19 years I have those that represents the nine rings."

In terms of his favorite movies or TV shows, I asked him if there was a favorite movie or show that motivated him to drop everything he was doing at the moment and sit down and watch the rest of it?

"Hoosiers, Remember the Titans," he said. "As for TV shows, I love "The Mentalist."

His range was impressive, yet Drew proceeded to go to the next level, not settling for just one category while adding more favorites.

"I like Person of Interest, and I'm a Saturday Night Live guy."

I told him we needed to get him on SNL.

"We'll have to see if I have the 'range' to ever get on?" he said. Stay tuned. He works for NBC now.

For perspective, one year I asked Drew, who had enjoyed such a rare long career, if he could pick a former NFL player as his teammate, who would it be? He went straight to a reference from his mentor.

"I remember Doug Flutie talking about Walter Payton a lot and just what a great teammate he was, what a great man he was," Drew said. "There's just one degree of separation there which is kind of interesting, I played with Doug Flutie, and his first TD pass was to Walter Payton."

Behind the scenes, Drew could adeptly answer any question, and he also learned to deal with something that Flutie and Walter didn't: social media. During one of our lengthy interview sessions, I delved into that growing dynamic and how he perceived it, asking "When you came into the league in 2001, you didn't have Facebook, Instagram, or Twitter. How has this changed the dynamics of being a pro athlete and a high-profile NFL quarterback?

"It's not necessarily the social media, because you can choose to tune that out," he said. "it's probably just the access to it, it's the phones. Yeah, I had cell phones in the locker room when I was a young player, but it wasn't until my junior year of college that cell phones could be something that people could walk around with, right? Or it was like you're carrying it in a briefcase."

Drew understood the effects of modern technology and how it impacted those younger teammates in his locker room.

"Young players are so locked into their phones," he said. "You even see it with kids nowadays. It's one of those things I'm trying to wrap my head around in-regards- to my kids. It's like, at what age is it appropriate for them? And what are the rules when they do have one? I feel like we're losing so much of this interpersonal connection, and so we try to limit that as much as possible with our kids. I would say that's the different part, that's the part that I think is most important to create in a locker room is guys just wanting to be around each other."

The Saints quarterback acknowledged that the team made moves to improve overall communication in the later stages of his career.

"Having a ping pong table in our locker room is one of the best things to happen all year," he said. "No joke because we'll have 10 to 12 guys just rallied around the ping pong table while two guys are playing. Guys are jawing with each other, guys are having a good time, but it's that connection, guys are laughing. You are just enjoying that time with each other as opposed to (picks up his hand like he's lifting a cell phone) being locked in on what's going on your Facebook, your social media, who's tweeting you or who you're tweeting, or whatever it might be."

Drew is active on his social media platforms, where you can routinely see him posting on his Twitter or Instagram accounts. "Listen, there is a time and place for that, and I think it's a great way to connect with the fans, a great way to get information, and so if you use it for that when the time is right it's great," he said. "But man, when you're in the locker room,

I feel like that's the time to be with the fellas, that's the time to build team chemistry."

For many professional athletes, Twitter began as a platform that encouraged unprecedented fan interaction. But these days it's morphed into a vehicle where anyone can and often will freely criticize players. I wondered how hard it's been to deal with such criticism and has Drew paid much attention to his social media critics?

"Honestly, I don't have the time to scroll through my (timeline)," he said. "But I'll be honest with you, I'd say for the most part it's very positive. But I think some people use social media as their opportunity to say something that they want to say, hiding behind the screen."

It's not like he doesn't see the good with the bad, though as Drew admits, he does try to reach out to his followers when something on social media stands out.

"I like it when, every now and then, I'll jump on there and shoot something back to a fan," he said. "It could be in-regards to anything, football, life, whatever. It's fun to have that personal connection, I want those fans to feel like, especially if they're coming to me with a question and it's positive, I'm gonna be receptive to that."

With over a million followers on Twitter and seemingly thousands of responses and likes to every post, what specifically gets Drew's attention?

"When people talk about their kids, because I obviously post a lot of stuff about my kids, stuff I'm doing with them and this and that," he said. "(It could be) something funny they did, and somebody else will go on there and say my son did the same thing. My daughter said this when she was two, so that's fun. That's just trading real-life stories. I think a lot of times people think that because you're a professional football player or something that you kind of have this totally different life. Certain aspects of it are different, but the majority of it, man, I'm a dad, a father of four, a husband trying to be the same thing that many people are. I'm trying to have that purpose in life, trying to be the best person I can be, and I have some of the same struggles, same challenges, same experiences, and it's fun to be able to share that in this open forum, which I think is the best aspect of social media, that people can kind of go back and forth sharing that stuff with each other."

Drew knows how he deals with social media, but I wondered how he felt about the growing phenomenon of athletes routinely making news by what they post on their respective social media accounts in favor of what they used to just share face to face with the media? Some are much more active than others, so I asked him, "In terms of what we do, maybe some athletes don't want to talk to the media and will just tweet something out instead. That's their way of communicating. How has this dynamic changed for players who can just do that and not talk to the media? Is that's a different outlet for them now?

"Yeah, it is" he said. "And you know what, maybe that's not such a bad thing at times because they can choose their words wisely, and they can say it exactly the way they want to say it. Even though you can't feel the inflections sometimes, just the way you're writing something or the context, but it allows them, instead of just being reactionary to a question or whatever, they can sit there and think it out and just put it down the way they want and hit send."

Drew understands that NFL locker rooms contain a melting pot of personalities where the players will handle online messaging differently.

"Yeah, there's some reactionary stuff put out there obviously," he said. "I don't think you want to be in a position where you're going back and having to apologize for something. I think some guys feel more comfortable doing that (social media) than being in front of a camera or being asked a direct question like that. They kind of want to do it in their own way, on their own time."

From social media to endless hypotheticals, I tried to stump Drew for years with endless questions, but in our last official interview, I pulled out the heavy artillery to see if he could perfect the two-minute TV drill with the same veracity as he executed it within Sean Payton's offense. So, in our retirement special, I set the clock at two minutes and challenged Drew to answer ten questions in the allotted time. As usual, he didn't skip a beat, answering the barrage of questions without much hesitation:

Which former player would you have wanted as a teammate?

"John Lynch," Drew replied.

Who is the toughest player you ever faced?

"Zach Thomas."

How many more years will Tom Brady play?

"Two, maybe one."

You and your wife Brittany went to Iceland recently with friends. What remains on your travel bucket list?

He responded quickly, seemingly knowing what the question would be before I asked it, "Antarctica, the Galápagos Islands, Eastern Europe, Ukraine." I had to stop him as we had more questions to ask in this rapid-fire segment??

What would your advice be to Arch Manning (grandson of Archie Manning and nephew to Eli and Peyton), arguably the hottest high school quarterback prospect in the country?

After a quick pause, he countered with, "Be yourself and blaze your own trail."

What is your favorite current TV show?

"I just finished the Queen's Gambit. Really good on Netflix."

What is your go-to snack?

"Fritos and Hummus."

Who would play Drew Brees if they made a movie about your life?

After a rare pause, Drew jumped in and then called an audible. "I would have to say Matthew McConaughey" he said but then immediately went for option two, "but I'm gonna go a little more action and say, Jason Statham," opting with the Fast and Furious star over his fellow Texan buddy.

So, with :33 seconds left, Drew was in the driver's seat to meet his final two-minute challenge. If not the NFL, which career would you seek, the MLB or the PGA tour? Drew's reaction showed this may have been the most challenging question.

"Oh man, really tough, but I'd play Major League Baseball and then Senior Tour." The quarterback was proud of that response winking at the camera.

With less than :20 seconds left, I saved the best for last, asking him, "You will be in the Hall of Fame in five years. Who will introduce you? Will it be a family member, a teammate, a coach or... me?"

Drew immediately started laughing, where you could see the wheels truly turning in this head. Was this the moment that I finally had stumped him, or was it an instance where he didn't want to answer the question?

It was the latter.

"I'm gonna let it time out on that one," he said, pointing to the two-minute timer on the screen.

The clock had officially run out for me and Brees. I had saved my best for last, and finally, finally, I had stumped him.

It only took 14 years!

8

Extending His Prime

Drew handled his press conferences the way he sized up his weekly game plan, pregame chants and training protocol: measured and meticulous. While he routinely provided great answers, Drew rarely supplied any juicy replies that would warrant front-page headlines.

Then, in July of 2014, he delivered the exception to the rule. At 35, Drew arrived at the Saints' new training camp digs at the luxurious Greenbrier in West Virginia with an unexpected proclamation. He wanted to play another ten years.

"I'm serious. I'm not delusional, " he said in his first media gathering of the Saints preseason. "I know that's something that would be extremely difficult to do, not many have done it. It could be done but a lot of things would have to fall into place."

The statement at the time was shocking, especially for Drew. But his football mindset never wavered. The goal was always to maximize his time in the NFL. He wanted to squeeze every second possible out of his football life. During the years I covered Drew, he seldom if ever talked about retire-ment. Instead, he was constantly planning what was next. He never wanted his career to end.

Four years after making that statement, while on the cusp of turning 40, Drew told me in 2018, "Everybody made a big deal of the playing-till-I'm-45 statement. I was in one of those really enthusiastic moods and just kind of threw it out there, knowing I would get that effect. I'm not naïve. I know it's a grind, so I really just take it one day at a time, one game at a time, one season at a time."

Perhaps, but in retrospect Drew was confident in making the state-ment because of all the hard work he had put in with longtime trainer Todd Durkin and performance coach Tom House. "I feel my physical abilities have maintained," he said. "I feel like I can do just about everything I could do at age 25, but the difference is I'm just that much more experienced." His experience translated into confidence in his longevity. "So I've seen a lot of football, played a lot of football, prepared for a lot of football, been in a lot of situations. A lot of confidence comes along with that when I step on the field in-regards-to what I'm gonna see, what the defense might throw at me."

A few months after making that statement, Drew shared with me some of the motivation behind it. It came during the offseason from a fellow Texan and one of his boyhood idols, Nolan Ryan. "One of the things that kind of crossed my path during the month of July (2014) was kind of the career of Nolan Ryan," Drew said. "His last pitch at the age of 47, he threw it 95 miles an hour. You gotta shake your head at that. The guy had a 28-year professional career. It was incredible what he was able to kind of sustain throughout his career, and so you look at a guy like that in that day and age, and you say, 'Why not? why not play this career for that amount of time?'"

At the age of 35, Drew, motivated by the Ryan Express, was determined to keep his longtime routine going so that he would never have to look back and feel as if he could have trained harder or taken better care of his body. "I've heard a lot of NFL quarterbacks and major league pitchers say that they would have kept on playing and pitching but they just couldn't do the five-day turnaround as a starting pitcher in the major leagues or do the seven-day turnaround to play another NFL football game. Had they been given two weeks, they could have done it, and they would have done it."

A big part of Drew's belief that he could extend his career for another decade stemmed from the fact he had already surpassed his own expectations. "When I first got into the league, it was, 'Gosh, I just want to be a starting quarterback in the NFL. Wouldn't that be something?' Instead, I'm a second-round pick sitting behind Doug Flutie in San Diego. In the second year I get to compete and now I'm a starting quarterback."

After earning the starting spot, Drew gradually realized how much more of an impact he could make at the NFL level. "And then it was like, 'OK, now that I'm a starting quarterback. I want to be a really good one. I'd like to be a Pro-Bowl starting quarterback.' That would be a great level of respect and certainly a great accomplishment."

The grind paid off as Drew's play improved. So did his confidence in terms of the places he could take his career. "A couple of years later, I make it to the Pro Bowl, and so then I started thinking, 'How long can I make it, how long can I stick around in this game? If I get to double digits, that would be something.' Then, at age 32, I hit double digits. So now, it's kind of 'Well, what's next? Let's get to 35.' And once you're at 35, it's like, 'Alright, let's really sit here and think what we can do.'"

At 35, Drew felt optimistic about his football future because, every year, he would see his skills maintained while many of his peers would slowly ride off into retirement. In 2017, I asked him how the recent retirement of former Saints teammate Reggie Bush made him feel and if it allowed him to put into perspective the great extended career that he was enjoying? "Yeah, that (referring to Bush) and I'll tell you what was strange watching LaDainian Tomlinson go into the Hall of Fame this year (2017), we were in the same class in San Diego in 2001," Drew told me.

Watching former teammates retire and go into the Hall was one thing, but Drew took it a step further, "There are five guys on our coaching staff that I played against, one in college and the others in the NFL," he said. Does that make you feel good, I asked?

"You play long enough, yeah, it gives you a ton of history to reference, tons of memories," he said. "When it's all said and done, looking back on the times with those guys, their careers, and the things you were able to accomplish together."

Enjoying a long career just fueled Drew to want more. The mindset to play as long as he could was put to the test in his final two seasons, when he missed extended time for the first time in his career. First, in 2019, he suffered a thumb injury. Weeks later, (for the first time in our 14 years together and frankly for the first time publicly,) Drew unveiled the aforementioned yet poignant "two" words to me in an interview. The words "borrowed time," which were an honest admission of how he approached the game at that juncture of his career. He wanted to savor every moment and didn't want to leave any opportunities on the table. It was that mindset that fueled his decision to come back a week before a bye week that would have given him more time to nurse the thumb injury. Playing on what he perceived to be "borrowed time" pushed him to come back early so that he would never regret missing any games that he could have potentially played.

Drew's borrowed time mindset evolved into a new phrase, "extending his prime." That was the thought process he employed to help him push his career into his 40s, an era he never imagined possible when he first broke into the league. I first heard of his "extending his prime" mantra when I interviewed Drew during his injury-plagued 2019 season. I asked him if experience was now allowing him to do things as a quarterback that he couldn't do five or ten years earlier? "Your ability to play at a high level into your later years is to me, I define that as saying I'm extending my prime," Drew said. "I'm trying to extend my prime. I'm trying to stay in my prime as long as I can."

It was the first time I heard Drew express how he was approaching the maturation of his career in those terms. It was just weeks after I first heard him say he was playing on "borrowed time." It was evident that he knew the clock was ticking on his Hall of Fame career, and the only way to reach his goal of extending his prime was to evolve in terms of the physical and mental aspects of his game. "What is your prime? To me, my prime is where your physical abilities are at a maximum level and then your mental abilities, what you've learned, what you've developed, your experience, that wisdom that kind of gets up to a certain level." Drew said. Then moving his hands as if he's building his pillar of excellence, he said, "Then you're just able to maintain that. At some point, I think you're mental, and your wisdom continues to go upright because the more that you experience, the more that you gain, right? And then, at some point, the aging process kicks in and that physical wants to drop. I think a lot of guys call it quits. That's when they retire."

For Drew, the opportunity to extend his prime had a shelf life for everyone, even him. But as long as this mindset worked, he would continue to play. He felt he knew what the secret sauce was. "If you can maintain that physical along with that mental, you're maintaining your prime," he said. "And for me, that's what beating the aging process is, and that's what I feel like. The experience and the wisdom continues to grow with every snap." As he explained this thought process, Drew grew excited, knowing all of his past experiences only helped him maintain his current level of play. "If I can process something that much faster (he snaps his finger) than I did a couple years ago or get to that check (he snaps his fingers again) that much faster than a couple of years ago, that might be the difference between that big play, something that sustains drives, something that scores points, something that wins games," he told me.

At the age of 35, Drew was eager to play ten more years, but he found later in his career that he wanted to make another significant adjustment. He tried to enjoy the game and all it gave back. Drew repeatedly admitted that he increasingly enjoyed the little things more in his last few years, the plane rides home after victories and the postgame celebrations with his teammates. He didn't want to look back and regret not appreciating those little things. Talking to former players who had failed to soak it all in sparked that adjustment. "I hear from guys, when they leave this game, they miss the locker room, they miss that game day experience, the journey, the experiences," he said. "I don't want it to pass me by, I want to enjoy the moment."

Drew's appreciation of the game was something he tried to pass on to a Saints team that continued to grow younger than its star quarterback. "I try to install that confidence in my teammates as well," he said. "I'm just having fun and really just taking it one opportunity at a time 'cause I don't ever want to lose track of the moment. I just want to stay in the moment as much as I can." I asked, Did being older help?

Drew smiled and referred to the adage of old age and treachery will always beat youth and exuberance. "Yes, old age wisdom and treachery," he said.

Drew's mindset coincided with not only his peers heading into retirement but stars he had entered the professional limelight with, such as Derek Jeter, Jeff Gordon, and Kobe Bryant, the latter of whom retired in 2016 when he was just a year older than Brees. The Saints quarterback told me at the time, "Yeah, while you're in it, you're just grinding away. It's one game at a time, one season at a time and you're not even thinking about the end. You're not thinking about it. It's not even a blip on the radar. Then all of these guys start to retire, the ones you mentioned, and you begin to say, 'I remember when that guy got in the league (smiling). It was about the same time I got in the league.' So that kind of put things into perspective a little bit as to I've been able to play a long time. That's a blessing."

The extending his prime mantra worked for Drew, who played a re-markable 20 seasons in the NFL. During his time with me, Drew seldom speculated about retirement. He ultimately told me the plan was to retire when he felt the time was right. "My goal is to walk away from this game even when I have good years left," he said. "I don't want to walk away when the Saints say they don't want me anymore, or because there are 32 teams that say they don't want me. I want to go out on my terms, and when I do, I'll tell you right now, it will be to spend more time with my family. It will be to be more present as a husband and a father, to coach my kids and be even more a part of their life."

Drew said that years before his last game, that playoff loss to the Buc-caneers in 2021. He knew it was over while he stood with his wife Brittany as they watched their kids play football together in the Superdome. He was still soaking up every moment, leaving the game on his terms, just the way he had predicted, indeed, the way he had planned, several years prior. "Listen, the season takes its toll, it takes a lot of time, a lot of physical energy, a lot of emotional energy," he said then. "When I walk away, it will be to spend more time with my family, and hopefully, I'm the one making that call."

He did make that call, a rarity in his line of work.

Retirement, Broadcasting Brees

(AND BEYOND)

For years, the fans, the media, even many players and coaches around the NFL wondered when the Drew Brees era would end? You knew the Saints magic carpet ride had to conclude at some point, and it did on March 14th, 2021, via an Instagram post. Drew made it official with the help of a creative video from all four of his kids, who expressed their excitement.

Brees' youngest son Callen emphasized, "Finally," and then all four punctuated the announcement with "So he can spend more time with us." Followed by a big cheer as in unison they collectively jumped off their living room couch in excitement. Previously, this announcement would have come as a shock. This time, it was a foregone conclusion. The only surprise was that it took months instead of weeks for the news to become official. Drew picked his spot, waiting until the exact date (March 14th) that he originally signed with the Saints 15 years earlier.

A few months later, Drew told me he had seen the end coming for years.

"I think I've recognized that over the last few years, it was coming," he said. "Since 2017, I was truly taking it one year at a time as if this could be my last season. At the end of each season, it was, 'Alright. What do I have left in the tank? What needs to be done?' And then I think just an overall feeling of whether it's time or not."

By 2021, injuries had taken their toll, and with his family getting older, the Saints' icon knew the time was right to walk away.

"I think this time around, having played 20 seasons and just knowing where my kids are and that I want to be a part of moving forward, I knew it was time."

Drew knew the timing was right but admitted it was a strange feeling approaching an offseason and ultimately a July without the mindset he had to gear up for a football season. It was the first time since he put on the pads as a freshman in high school in Austin, Texas, in 1992 that he went into the late summer not preparing for a season of football.

Since announcing his retirement, Drew has taken on many new hobbies to replace football, including riding an electric bike, fishing, surfing, even woodworking. I asked how strange it was, even though he was enjoying his retirement, that he wasn't preparing to play football in the fall or prepping for another physical and hot preseason?

"All of this has snuck up on me," he said. "It's pretty wild, but at the same time, it's pretty refreshing not to get out there in that heat and suffer like you do in training camp."

The best player to ever put on a Saints uniform wasn't struggling to stay busy yet he realized football will always be a part of his life.

"It's hard to get too far from the game," he said. "I managed to keep up with a lot of teammates during the offseason and had a chance to be around the Saints facility as well."

Over the years, I picked and prodded Drew on what he would do when he finally would wave goodbye to the game he had played for decades. In 2015, for example, I asked him if he could look into a crystal ball, what would he be doing in 15 years? No surprise, his mind focused not on him but on his family.

"First thing I'm gonna say is, how hold are my kids?" he replied while immediately extending his hands and counting. "So we'll have a 21-, 20-, 18-, and 16-year old. Now, the 16-year-old will be Rylen, my baby girl, starting to drive, so I'll be a basket case is what I'll be. I'll be in a mental institution."

We both laughed, but it was clear Drew was struggling with the notion that one day, his kids will be older, out of the house, and he will no longer be playing the game he loves.

"Fifteen years will be a long time," he told me. "Brittney and I will be empty nesters at that point. I think we'll have some pretty elaborate travel plans all kind of laid out and just be looking forward to every holiday on the books. Thanksgiving, Christmas, Easter, when all the kids come home and bring their significant others, that kind of thing. That will be a whole new adventure."

Drew was right. Forecasting your life 15 years in advance can be a tricky proposition. A lot can happen in that time. But the truth is, as much as he didn't want to talk about when his playing career would end, he did a good job preparing for when that tough day would come. His mentor Doug Flutie serves as a great example of making a successful transition as he has found a busy life after football. He offered his understudy this post-football advice.

"I think the number one thing is find something your passionate in, find something that gets you excited the way football got you excited," Flutie relayed from experience currently in his baseball uniform ready to hit the field for his latest game.

Flutie appreciated that Drew had built quite a diverse set of business interests to set himself up after his playing days.

"He's done great business-wise," Flutie said. "He started his Walk-On's, all his Jimmy John's, and all that stuff he owns, so he's been in the right direction for a long time."

Flutie's final piece of advice was very revealing: "Money is not the issue," he said. "What you need is something that motivates you on a regular basis, so you want to be great at it."

Drew, like Flutie, will take his competitive fire from the huddle to any future enterprise. He told Reuters in 2011 that running for public office is something he would likely consider.

"Definitely, politics fascinates me," Drew said. "I find it very interesting. I guess, when you look at all the issues and certainly in the current economic times, at times you hate to see both parties going at each other like they do."

In this interview, Drew didn't merely flirt with the idea of being a politician one day. You could tell he had some passion when it came to both the process and its overall impact.

"You feel at times, this is counter-productive," he added. "Why can't we just stick to the issues? Why can't we just work to resolve some of the problems that our country has and the rest of the global economy has and (focus on) ways that we can help?"

The former quarterback knew he couldn't win on the football field by himself and understands that mindset will follow him if he someday runs for an elected office.

"I think the fact that anybody who goes into politics feels like, 'I can make a difference,'" he said. "But It's not one person. You need so many others. I would love to do it, probably at some point, but I'll wait a while. I'd consider it. I am not going to close any doors, hopefully, that's some time away."

Drew's thoughts on a career in politics came ten years before he would walk away from football, but frankly, I thought he was going to retire a year before he announced it. Having done hundreds of interviews with him, Drew always gives thoughtful answers but is smart enough not to let you inside on many fronts. Understandably, he's private regarding his family. In addition, he doesn't reveal details of his workout routine, and overall, he is cordial yet neutral when talking about his opponents and his thoughts on his career.

But when I asked him at the 2019 Pro Bowl about his thoughts of becoming a broadcaster, I was surprised by the degree of passion the subject evoked. Years prior, Drew had told me that one day, he would love to be a college football analyst, not just because he would enjoy doing the job but because he could take his kids on the road with him and allow them to take in the whole experience. This time my questions about broadcasting sparked more emotion. I sensed he had several networks offers on the table, which it turned out he did. At the 2019 Pro Bowl, I reminded him of his comments from years prior on his desire to become a college analyst so he could take his kids on the road with him and asked again, could you see yourself as a broadcaster?

"Sure, I love the game," he said. "I feel I see the game from a different perspective than most people do. I can anticipate things, you know, just based on my knowledge (of) these players, these opponents, these coaches, these teams. And so I think that I could bring great value and great perspective in that way."

Drew conveyed rare outward confidence to me on an expertise away from football where he not only felt he could be a good broadcaster but would enjoy the job, too.

"I think it would be a lot of fun," he said. "It would be a way to feel like you were playing the game without playing the game because you're sitting there each step of the game anticipating, calling, verbalizing, explaining. So all of that sounds very interesting to me, and I think I could be good at it."

At that moment, I thought Drew was going to take a network job and retire. He rarely is that candid in his feelings on anything he does, yet admitted broadcasting would be the perfect fit for him. A few days later, NBC Sports announced they had hired him as an analyst for college football games and had him joining an all-star cast on the network's critically acclaimed Football Night in America team. For years, ESPN had been looking for a big name to replace Jon Gruden as an analyst, so you knew Drew would create a bidding war for his services if he had the interest. Clearly, at that moment, he had caught the broadcasting bug, so frankly, I was surprised a few weeks later, in February of 2020, when he announced he would be coming back for what would be his final season. NBC simultaneously announced its offer would be waiting for Drew when he did eventually retire, which speaks volumes for how much they wanted him.

This move didn't come as a surprise to Roman Harper either. Harper saw Drew, the analyst before he officially aspired to be Drew, the analyst. The former Saints safety was playing in Carolina late in his career when he watched a game with his former quarterback at the home of Panthers' safety Kurt Coleman in Charlotte. Harper had never seen his former teammate in this sort of element and came away impressed with his TV potential.

"I've been around him watching football games, and you should hear him talk through a two-minute situation," Harper said. "It's awesome to like, really hear him dive into what he's thinking and really open up the mind of a great quarterback."

Harper said the fun part of hearing Drew break a game down is the intricate details he passes on from every vantage point.

"Oh, he sees it," Harper said, "Let's say the clock is running down and he's like telling the quarterback on TV, 'Hey, you still got plenty of time; you just want to get yards, you just want to get positive plays.' Just that mindset of a quarterback in a two-minute situation, it's really, really cool to see that, and I think if he continues to share those experiences with the fans, they'll love it too."

Zach Strief took a different post-football route to the broadcast booth. He made the unprecedented move from playing right tackle for the Saints to becoming the team's play-by-play man a year later. He concedes Drew has picked his brain about making the transition.

"We've talked about it a couple of times, actually," Strief said. "I've sent some stuff his way, ways that I did it, ways I prepared."

Strief wanted to help Drew in many ways, beginning with preparing for a telecast, which is different from constructing a game plan.

"I know that feeling of like, 'Ok, I've got this thing I have to do,' and he knows in football that's not an issue right, it's not about that, he knows how to prepare for that. You gotta find your way to do it. I always like to have things organized this way. Here's stats that come into play, and here's stats that don't."

Strief passed on to Drew a lesson he learned from veteran broadcaster Al Michaels on how to best communicate to the viewer.

"The great advice that I got from Al Michaels is, 'Nobody knows what the (heck) a three-technique is, so you gotta dumb things down a little bit; you have to simplify,'" Strief said. "That is what I think is gonna be one of his hardest things, and I shared as much with him."

With no previous broadcasting experience, Strief was an unlikely choice for the Saints play-by-play job. Like Brees, though, he is smart, a quick study. Those two traits will help the former Saints quarterback in his new career as well. But Strief knows a challenge for Drew will be condensing all the years of football knowledge he possesses into a convenient format to his viewers.

"He's gonna have so much information in his head that he's capable of sharing, but he doesn't have the time to share it all," Strief said. "So, learning that balance of, 'OK, this is something that I can explain and this is something that people will understand and knowing when it's time to explain something and when it's simply time to get it back to the play-by-play announcer.' Like those are the balancing acts that make great color commentators great."

Strief feels his former quarterback is more than capable, but he warns that the transition won't be easy.

"I do think there's gonna be a part of that again where he has to learn," Strief said. "He can very easily explain to you what coverage a defense was in and why they threw the route they threw. But the casual listener doesn't understand anything he just said. There's gonna be a balance there of picking and choosing some of that stuff."

Drew will never lose his competitive nature, not even in the broadcast booth. While converted analyst and former NFL quarterback Tony Romo has received rave reviews for his penchant for forecasting plays, many who know Drew feel surpassing Romo as the best color man will be his goal.

"He will never once say that, but he will always be thinking it; no no question; that's how he is," Strief said, believing Drew has every bit the same broadcasting potential as Romo. "Tony Romo has gotten famous for predicting plays. That's his signature. Well, Drew can do that constantly."

There is no doubt Drew will prepare, but how will he approach one of the tougher demands of being an analyst, the part of the job when you have to criticize the play or the poor behavior of players? At the Pro Bowl in 2020, I asked Drew if it would be hard to critique players you recently competed against on the field? It was one of the few times in our 14 years together that he took exception with one of my questions.

"I don't feel like you have to (criticize)," he said. "Why would you have to criticize guys?"

He didn't see this aspect of being an analyst that way. His approach to broadcasting was to not get personal like some color commentators. He prefers to frame it as constructive criticism. "I think you just lay out and explain it in a way that's not critical," Drew said.

For Brees, the broadcaster, the mindset in his new job would be not what you say but how you say it.

"Listen, some things, they are what they are," he said. "Like, I wish I had that throw back or whatever it is? I think more so than anything, it's a way to help fans. So I think it helps fans become more knowledgeable and enjoy the game even more."

Strief understands the dynamic of criticizing players from a media standpoint.

"I think there is a conscious, 'Ah, I don't wanna pound somebody' even though sometimes people deserve that," he said. But he also sees Drew's point of view.

"I think he's absolutely right," Strief continued. "There's a way to attack a problem and not a player and he's gonna know that, and he's gonna know and understand why something happened or why something didn't. I think that's really gonna be his strength. I think if you know Drew and the way that his process is for things like this, he's gonna prepare to understand what is supposed to happen and be able to share with listeners why it didn't, and I think that will be really fascinating. You know, I think that will be really good."

It's ironic how both Drew and his mentor Flutie's career paths played out in football and subsequently broadcasting. Before he signed his deal with NBC, Flutie had worked for the network in a similar capacity calling Notre Dame games and serving as an NFL analyst, but he didn't have the same zeal for broadcasting as Drew does.

"I've done the broadcasting thing, and I enjoyed it for a while, and I still do it, but I'm not anywhere as passionate about that as I am about football," Flutie said.

While Flutie gave Brees tons of advice early in his career on adapting to the pro game, he also has offered him perspective on how to adapt to the broadcasting game and the misnomers that come with it.

"It's a full-time job," Flutie said. "That's the problem. It's not just show up at the game and do it."

Flutie passed on to him the amount of work an analyst puts in but he has the same confidence in his protégé in the booth that he had in Drew on the field, beginning with preparation.

"It's game planning, it's watching film," Flutie said. "Drew was great at that, starting back in San Diego. For instance, he got his offensive lineman together for a night, and they would watch film and all that stuff. He started doing that at a young age, so he's got that in him. I think he does have the desire to be really good. He wants (to do well)."

Drew agreed with Flutie that a big draw of broadcasting was the chance to apply his passion for preparation in a different field. In addition, the challenge was something he could apply to both of his new roles in television.

"Studying tape, learning the disciplines that go with each of those broadcasting and in-studio (roles), you really do use different muscles," he said. "They are two really different animals."

As much as those two on-air positions were different, Drew recognized another big difference. He had a big learning curve when it came to an arena he used to know like the back of his hand but now had to reacquaint himself with.

"For me, it's an opportunity to really learn a great skill set with both (Notre Dame and Football Night in America)," he said. "I think the biggest challenge is probably gonna be learning the college game. I've been watching college football on Saturday nights on the road before games but (now I'm) learning the college football environment and learning a lot about the coaches and the players and the systems, obviously studying Notre Dame football quite a bit."

Learning the college game and the Irish is one thing, but Drew also knew he would have to take his pro knowledge to the next level.

"Also being very much attuned to what is happening in the NFL because that is what the hour and 12-minute show is devoted to with "Football Night in America," every Sunday night, it'll be fun," he said. "It'll definitely be an adjustment, it will be a challenge but a challenge I'm looking forward to."

After flirting with retirement following the 2019 season, Drew knew full well that 2020 would be his last go-round. His 20th season in 2020 would be with a team built to win, and even though injuries would hold him back, he admitted that he only felt 100 percent in one game all season, against Detroit in Week 4. He understood that having a career close to the game would make the transition easier, but leaving the game he loved for decades would never be easy.

"Oh, I know I'll miss it, and it's a big reason why I took advantage of the opportunity to sign with NBC," he said, "It's an opportunity to not only be a broadcaster for Notre Dame games with Mike Tirico and do the in-studio work for Football Night in America, but to stay connected with the game, the coaches and the players and (maintain) all those relationships I've been able to build throughout my career and just fill that void that I know will come by not being a player anymore."

Ex-players know, playing the game through the eyes of an analyst never replaces the feel of leading touchdown drives on Sundays. But for Drew the thought of being able to pass on his knowledge of the game while still being close to the action offers a similar reward.

"I'm excited for this next chapter, excited for this next opportunity," he said. "At the same time, I do recognize there will be challenges. There will be kind of a range of emotions, especially as we get closer to football season when you start getting that itch and that excitement knowing guys are going back to work and starting to prepare for another season and you're not part of it as a player anymore."

For Drew's teammates, many predict big things for him as a broadcaster, but they frankly see big things in anything he attempts.

"The things that make him exceptional translate to everything," Strief said. "A guy who has that level of work ethic and determination and intelligence and drive, it doesn't matter what he does. He's gonna be good at it."

It could be the media, politics, and for some, or it could be something you might not have guessed.

"Drew is the best leader I've ever been around, so for me, I think he will excel in any role he does. I think he could go to TV. He will give us his best as an analyst, there's no doubt," said former teammate and Saints linebacker Scott Shanle, who added a surprising endorsement. "But I also think this about Drew. I think Drew Brees is one of the few players who could go straight from being a player in the NFL to being one of the best head coaches in the NFL. I think he would be one of the best coaches the game has ever seen."

"I really think that highly of him in terms of him walking into a room and the ultimate respect being there. Everybody would play hard for him. He would motivate many quarterbacks with his status, go out and do a pregame chant for as many years as he does, come up with something new every single year, and everyone gets hyped before the game with their Super Bowl-winning future hall of fame quarterback? Those are the things Drew can do. He's a leader of men, but more importantly, as a leader, I think he should become a head coach someday," Shanle said.

"I could see where Shanle's coming from because Drew was always around, was always in the meeting room," Roman Harper said. "Those gym rats like that, they don't know what to do with themselves when they're no longer in the locker room, in that meeting room or grinding like they always have, so that will be something Drew will have to adjust to."

"I think he'd be a great coach because it's beyond the X's and O's," Lance Moore said, agreeing with his two former teammates. "It's being able to motivate guys, being able to talk the talk, right? He's been there. He's been to the plateau of the NFL, not just as an all-time leader in a lot of statistical categories but as an all-time leader as far as leadership goes. (He's been) the captain of a team, he's been to multiple Pro Bowls, won a Super Bowl and a Super Bowl MVP, so who wouldn't want to play for a guy like that or work for a guy like that? He's gonna be great at whatever he chooses to be. I believe that wholeheartedly."

Drew's teammates saw him lead them to many victories for years and forecast similar success in any endeavor he chooses post-football. "Would he be a good head coach? Absolutely, he'd be a great head coach," Strief said. "Would he be a good CEO of a company? Yeah, he would be great. There's all kinds of good attributes. I think he'll do well at anything."

Drew didn't slow down once he retired, immediately diving into broadcasting but also staying active with his foundation, his businesses, and all of the newfound hobbies he couldn't enjoy as an NFL quarterback.

"This is giving me the chance to get into other things that I otherwise wouldn't be doing, mountain biking, eFoiling some stuff that would not be in my contract," Drew said. "It's been fun to try some of that other stuff."

The former Saints quarterback is early in his post-football trek, but like Flutie, is wired to stay active and has put a premium on staying busy with his new routine.

"I still get up as early as I can, get my two cups of coffee, and try to get a bunch of work done before the kids get up, then be part of the get-ready-for-school process," he said. "Then I just try to keep myself busy until the kids get home and then it becomes trying to help coach football, basketball, baseball and just being involved in the kids' lives, having fun as a family."

One day his family will be out of the house, and Drew knows it. His future has many possibilities, and right now, he's just creating many options.

"What I'm kind of seeing, and this is no different than what most of us do, and I'm glad he's doing this because I think it's the right way is, he is absolutely burying himself in things," Strief said. "He's involved in everything. If you really watch, he's all over the place right now, and he's going to eventually find through experience the thing that fulfills him, and then he'll do that, and it might be a combination of things."

Drew was the vital cog in rebuilding both New Orleans and its football team. Now moving forward, he is seeking success at the next phase, whatever that turns out to be.

"We don't have experience in anything else," Strief said. "We're experts in one thing and one thing only, and then one day it's over, and you can't be an expert in it anymore. No one is gonna pay him to throw a football ever again, and he's spent his entire life optimizing his ability to throw that football, so that skill is out the window. So now you've got to start over."

The face of the Saints changed football forever in New Orleans, often making every right call inside the huddle. Now his life is located outside the huddle, where Drew still has many different play calls at his disposal.

"He is doing the right thing," Strief said. "He is surrounding himself with options and different things, and one of those will reveal itself to him as 'This is it, this is what I'm passionate about, what I love,' and it might be a combination of things. It might be two things. It's not going to be the seven things that are going on right now."

"There was a time two years ago where I would have told you I would be the voice of the Saints for the next 30 years, and it changed, it didn't happen, and I think he'll go through that same process because we all do. He's just fortunate that he's gonna have a lot of opportunities to do pretty much anything he wants."

ACKNOWLEDGMENTS

A sincere thanks to my bosses at Cox Sports Television, Rod Mickler and Jeff Brenner. Both have supported the efforts of this book and me in so many ways for several years.

I couldn't have done this project without the cooperation of Drew Brees and Chris Stuart, a partnership I will always appreciate. Thanks for your assistance, it meant a great deal.

To the Romig family, I enjoyed our enlightening zoom interview. You're a special group!

For my editor and longtime journalist Roy Cummings, you taught me a lot in this process. Your friendship and expertise were invaluable.

Longtime photographer Parker Waters' vintage Brees photos and stories were greatly appreciated.

I couldn't have put this project together without the creative talents of Kendra Cagle and the advice and direction of Janica Smith, thank you both!

ABOUT THE AUTHOR

Mike Nabors is an Emmy and Telly award winning broadcast journalist and national writer having covered every game of the Sean Payton/ Drew Brees era.

He's been an NFL reporter for over three decades in New Orleans, Tampa and Jacksonville. Mike's career includes being a longtime contributor to mlb.com and has served as the television host for the Tampa Bay Lightning and Fox Sports Net.

He can be reached at: **mnabors@naborsmediagroup.com**

CPSIA information can be obtained
at www.ICGtesting.com
Printed in the USA
BVHW052236181221
624451BV00016B/1466